Grade 3

Scott Foresman

Leveled Reader

Teaching Guide

PEARSON

Scott Foresman

Editorial Offices: Glenview, Illinois • Parsippany, New Jersey • New York, New York
Sales Offices: Boston, Massachusetts • Duluth, Georgia • Glenview, Illinois
Coppell, Texas • Sacramento, California • Mesa, Arizona

ISBN: 0-328-16915-3

5 6 7 8 9 10 V084 12 11 10 09 08 07

Table of Contents

LEVELED READER TITLE	Instruction	Comprehension Practice	Vocabulary Practice
Salt Lick Boom Town	12–13	14	15
Let's Make a Trade!	16–17	18	19
Let's Save Money!	20–21	22	23
Earning Money My Own Way	24–25	26	27
One Chili Pepper	28–29	30	31
Birds That Can't Fly!	32–33	34	35
The Boy Who Cried Wolf	36–37	38	39
Katy's Last-Minute Book Report	40–41	42	43
Our Garden	44–45	46	47
The Colonial Adventure	48–49	50	51
Tulips for Annie's Mother	52–53	54	55
Pictures in the Sky	56–57	58	59
The First Year	60–61	62	63
A Day with the Dogs	64–65	66	67
Mount St. Helens	68–69	70	71
Brave Settlers in a Strange Land	72–73	74	75
Getting the Lay of the Land	76–77	78	79
Fun With Science!	80–81	82	83

Graphic Organizers

Introduction

Scott Foresman *Reading Street* provides over 600 leveled readers that help children become better readers and build a lifelong love of reading. The *Reading Street* leveled readers are engaging texts that help children practice critical reading skills and strategies. They also provide opportunities to build vocabulary, understand concepts, and develop reading fluency.

The leveled readers were developed to be age-appropriate and appealing to children at each grade level. The leveled readers consist of engaging texts in a variety of genres, including fantasy, folk tales, realistic fiction, historical fiction, and narrative and expository nonfiction. To better address real-life reading skills that children will encounter in testing situations and beyond, a higher percentage of nonfiction texts is provided at each grade.

USING THE LEVELED READERS

You can use the leveled readers to meet the diverse needs of your children. Consider using the readers to

- practice critical skills and strategies
- build fluency
- build vocabulary and concepts
- build background for the main selections in the student book
- provide a variety of reading experiences, e.g., shared, group, individual, take-home, readers' theater

GUIDED READING APPROACH

The *Reading Street* leveled readers are leveled according to Guided Reading criteria by experts trained in Guided Reading. The Guided Reading levels increase in difficulty within a grade level and across grade levels. In addition to leveling according to Guided Reading criteria, the instruction provided in the *Leveled Reader Teaching Guide* is compatible with Guided Reading instruction. An instructional routine is provided for each leveled reader. This routine is most effective when working with individual children or small groups.

MANAGING THE CLASSROOM

When using the leveled readers with individuals or small groups, you'll want to keep the other children engaged in meaningful, independent learning tasks. Establishing independent work stations throughout the classroom and child routines for these work stations can help you manage the rest of the class while you work with individuals or small groups. Possible work stations include Listening, Phonics, Vocabulary, Independent Reading, and Cross-Curricular. For classroom management, create a work board that lists the work stations and which children should be at each station. Provide instructions at each station that detail the tasks to be accomplished. Update the board and alert children when they should rotate to a new station. For additional support for managing your classroom, see the *Reading Street Centers Survival Kit.*

USING THE LEVELED READER TEACHING GUIDE

The *Leveled Reader Teaching Guide* provides an instruction plan for each leveled reader based on the same instructional routine.

INTRODUCE THE BOOK The Introduction includes suggestions for creating interest in the text by discussing the title and author, building background, and previewing the book and its features.

READ THE BOOK Before students begin reading the book, have them set purposes for reading and discuss how they can use the reading strategy as they read. Determine how you want students in a particular group to read the text, softly or silently, to a specific point or the entire text. Then use the Comprehension Questions to provide support as needed and to assess comprehension.

REVISIT THE BOOK The Reader Response questions provide opportunities for students to demonstrate their understanding of the text, the target comprehension skill, and vocabulary. The Response Options require students to revisit the text to respond to what they've read and to move beyond the text to explore related content.

SKILL WORK The Skill Work box provides instruction and practice for the target skill and strategy and selection vocabulary. Instruction for an alternate comprehension skill allows teachers to provide additional skill instruction and practice for students.

USING THE GRAPHIC ORGANIZERS

Graphic organizers in blackline-master format can be found on pages 132–152. These can be used as overhead transparencies or as student worksheets.

ASSESSING PERFORMANCE

Use the assessment forms that begin on page 6 to make notes about your students' reading skills, use of reading strategies, and general reading behaviors.

MEASURE FLUENT READING (pp. 6–7) Provides directions for measuring a student's fluency, based on words correct per minute (wcpm), and reading accuracy using a running record.

OBSERVATION CHECKLIST (p. 8) Allows you to note the regularity with which students demonstrate their understanding and use of reading skills and strategies.

STUDENT SELF-ASSESSMENT (p. 9) Helps students identify their own areas of strength and areas where they need further work. This form (About My Reading) encourages them to list steps they can take to become better readers and to set goals as readers. Suggest that students share their self-assessment notes with their families so that family members can work with them more effectively to practice their reading skills and strategies at home.

READING STRATEGY ASSESSMENT (p. 10) Provides criteria for evaluating each student's proficiency as a strategic reader.

PROGRESS REPORT (p. 11) Provides a means to track a student's book-reading progress over a period of time by noting the level at which a student reads and his or her accuracy at that level. Reading the chart from left to right gives you a visual model of how quickly a student is making the transition from one level to the next. Share these reports with parents or guardians to help them see how their child's reading is progressing.

Measure Fluent Reading

Taking a Running Record

A running record is an assessment of a student's oral reading accuracy and oral reading fluency. Reading accuracy is based on the number of words read correctly. Reading fluency is based on the reading rate (the number of words correct per minute) and the degree to which a student reads with a "natural flow."

How to Measure Reading Accuracy

1. Choose a grade-level text of about 80 to 120 words that is unfamiliar to the student.
2. Make a copy of the text for yourself. Make a copy for the student or have the student read aloud from a book.
3. Give the student the text and have the student read aloud. (You may wish to record the student's reading for later evaluation.)
4. On your copy of the text, mark any miscues or errors the student makes while reading. See the running record sample on page 7, which shows how to identify and mark miscues.
5. Count the total number of words in the text and the total number of errors made by the student. Note: If a student makes the same error more than once, such as mispronouncing the same word multiple times, count it as one error. Self-corrections do not count as actual errors. Use the following formula to calculate the percentage score, or accuracy rate:

$$\frac{\text{Total Number of Words} - \text{Total Number of Errors}}{\text{Total Number of Words}} \times 100 = \text{percentage score}$$

Interpreting the Results

- A student who reads **95–100%** of the words correctly is reading at an **independent level** and may need more challenging text.
- A student who reads **90–94%** of the words correctly is reading at an **instructional level** and will likely benefit from guided instruction.
- A student who reads **89%** or fewer of the words correctly is reading at a **frustrational level** and may benefit most from targeted instruction with lower-level texts and intervention.

How to Measure Reading Rate (wcpm)

1. Follow Steps 1–3 above.
2. Note the exact times when the student begins and finishes reading.
3. Use the following formula to calculate the number of words correct per minute (wcpm):

$$\frac{\text{Total Number of Words Read Correctly}}{\text{Total Number of Seconds}} \times 60 = \text{words correct per minute}$$

Interpreting the Results

By the end of the year, a third-grader should be reading approximately 110–120 wcpm.

Running Record Sample

Running Record Sample

Dana had recently begun volunteering at the animal rescue shelter where her mom worked as a veterinarian. The shelter was (just) across the bay from their house.

Dana was learning many different [H] jobs at the shelter. She fed the dogs and cleaned their cages. She played catch with the dogs in the shelter's backyard. Dana's favorite /jŏb/ job, however, was introducing people to the dogs waiting for adoption. Whenever a dog found a new home, Dana was especially (sc) pleased!

The road to the shelter crossed over the bay. Dana looked for *the* boats in the channel, but there were none. Dana's mom turned on the radio to listen *hear* to the news as they drove. The weather reporter announced that a blizzard might hit some parts of the state.

—From *A Day with the Dogs*
On-Level Reader 3.3.4

Notations

Accurate Reading
The student reads a word correctly.

Omission
The student omits words or word parts.

Hesitation
The student hesitates over a word, and the teacher provides the word. Wait several seconds before telling the student what the word is.

Mispronunciation/Misreading
The student pronounces or reads a word incorrectly.

Self-correction
The student reads a word incorrectly but then corrects the error. Do not count self-corrections as actual errors. However, noting self-corrections will help you identify words the student finds difficult.

Insertion
The student inserts words or parts of words that are not in the text.

Substitution
The student substitutes words or parts of words for the words in the text.

Running Record Results
Total Number of Words: **126**
Number of Errors: **5**

Reading Time: **64 seconds**

▶ **Reading Accuracy**
$$\frac{126 - 5}{126} \times 100 = 96.032 = 96\%$$

Accuracy Percentage Score: **96%**

▶ **Reading Rate—WCPM**
$$\frac{121}{64} \times 60 = 113.44 = 113 \text{ words correct per minute}$$

Reading Rate: **113 WCPM**

Observation Checklist

Student's Name _____ Date _____

Behaviors Observed	Always (Proficient)	Usually (Fluent)	Sometimes (Developing)	Rarely (Novice)
Reading Strategies and Skills				
Uses prior knowledge and preview to understand what book is about				
Makes predictions and checks them while reading				
Uses context clues to figure out meanings of new words				
Uses phonics and syllabication to decode words				
Self-corrects while reading				
Reads at an appropriate reading rate				
Reads with appropriate intonation and stress				
Uses fix-up strategies				
Identifies story elements: character, setting, plot, theme				
Summarizes plot or main ideas accurately				
Uses target comprehension skill to understand the text better				
Responds thoughtfully about the text				

Reading Behaviors and Attitudes

	Always (Proficient)	Usually (Fluent)	Sometimes (Developing)	Rarely (Novice)
Enjoys listening to stories				
Chooses reading as a free-time activity				
Reads with sustained interest and attention				
Participates in discussion about books				

General Comments

© Pearson Education

About My Reading

Name _____ Date _____

1. Compared with earlier in the year, I am enjoying reading

   ☐ more   ☐ less   ☐ about the same

2. When I read now, I understand

   ☐ more than I used to   ☐ about the same as I used to

3. One thing that has helped me with my reading is

   _____

   _____

   _____

4. One thing that could make me a better reader is

   _____

   _____

   _____

5. Here is one selection or book that I really enjoyed reading:

   _____

   _____

6. Here are some reasons why I liked it:

   _____

   _____

   _____

   _____

   _____

Reading Strategy Assessment

Student _____ Date _____

Teacher _____

		Proficient	Developing	Emerging	Not showing trait
Building Background Comments:	Previews	☐	☐	☐	☐
	Asks questions	☐	☐	☐	☐
	Predicts	☐	☐	☐	☐
	Activates prior knowledge	☐	☐	☐	☐
	Sets own purposes for reading	☐	☐	☐	☐
	Other:	☐	☐	☐	☐
Comprehension Comments:	Retells/summarizes	☐	☐	☐	☐
	Questions, evaluates ideas	☐	☐	☐	☐
	Relates to self/other texts	☐	☐	☐	☐
	Paraphrases	☐	☐	☐	☐
	Rereads/reads ahead for meaning	☐	☐	☐	☐
	Visualizes	☐	☐	☐	☐
	Uses decoding strategies	☐	☐	☐	☐
	Uses vocabulary strategies	☐	☐	☐	☐
	Understands key ideas of a text	☐	☐	☐	☐
	Other:	☐	☐	☐	☐
Fluency Comments:	Adjusts reading rate	☐	☐	☐	☐
	Reads for accuracy	☐	☐	☐	☐
	Uses expression	☐	☐	☐	☐
	Other:	☐	☐	☐	☐
Connections Comments:	Relates text to self	☐	☐	☐	☐
	Relates text to text	☐	☐	☐	☐
	Relates text to world	☐	☐	☐	☐
	Other:	☐	☐	☐	☐
Self-Assessment Comments:	Is aware of: Strengths	☐	☐	☐	☐
	Needs	☐	☐	☐	☐
	Improvement/achievement	☐	☐	☐	☐
	Sets and implements learning goals	☐	☐	☐	☐
	Maintains logs, records, portfolio	☐	☐	☐	☐
	Works with others	☐	☐	☐	☐
	Shares ideas and materials	☐	☐	☐	☐
	Other:	☐	☐	☐	☐

Progress Report

Student's Name _____

At the top of the chart, record the book title, its grade/unit/week (for example, 1.2.3), and the student's accuracy percentage. See page 6 for measuring fluency, calculating accuracy and reading rates. At the bottom of the chart, record the date you took the running record. In the middle of the chart, make an X in the box across from the level of the student's reading—frustrational level (below 89% accuracy), instructional level (90–94% accuracy), or independent level (95–100% accuracy). Record the reading rate (WCPM) in the next row.

Book Title						
Grade/Unit/Week						
Reading Accuracy Percentage						
LEVEL **Frustrational** (89% or below)						
Instructional (90–94%)						
Independent (95% or above)						
Reading Rate (WCPM)						
Date						

Salt Lick Boom Town

SUMMARY Shelley the turtle discovers a tasty salt lick, and soon word spreads to animals everywhere. They come to lick the salt, and a boom town is born. Eventually, the animals lick away the salt and leave the bustling community. A ghost town is all that's left.

LESSON VOCABULARY

boom	coins
fetched	laundry
mending	pick
skillet	spell

INTRODUCE THE BOOK

INTRODUCE THE TITLE AND AUTHOR Discuss with students the title and the author of *Salt Lick Boom Town*. Ask them to look at the cover illustration and talk about how it might relate to the title. Who are the animals on the lower left, and what are they looking at?

BUILD BACKGROUND Ask: Do you know what a salt lick is? Why might animals flock to see a salt lick? Discuss reasons why towns and cities grow where they do. Ask: Why might a town become deserted?

ELL Tell students that this story focuses on an imaginary town. Help them find words from their native languages that mean the same as *boom town* and *ghost town*. Also discuss the differences between a small town, the suburbs, and a city.

PREVIEW/USE TEXT FEATURES Have students preview the book by looking at the illustrations. Point out that there are no photographs in the story. Ask: Why do you think the author used illustrations rather than photos? Have students look at page 16, which describes the features of a successful community. Ask students why they think this page looks different.

READ THE BOOK

SET PURPOSE Have students set a purpose for reading *Salt Lick Boom Town*. Invite them to ask questions about the title, such as, "What is a salt lick?" and "What is a boom town?" Students' curiosity about these topics should guide their purpose.

STRATEGY SUPPORT: PRIOR KNOWLEDGE Remind students that *prior knowledge* is what they know about a given topic and is gathered from their reading and personal experiences. Students living in big cities or large suburbs may not be familiar with a salt lick, but they may understand the concept of a boom town. Similarly, students with experience with farm animals may know what a salt lick is but may not understand the concept of a boom town. Help students see that people bring different kinds of prior knowledge and experience to their reading.

COMPREHENSION QUESTIONS

PAGE 4 What happens on this page to make it clear this story is a fantasy? (*Fuzzy the horse rides by on a bicycle.*)

PAGE 6 Is it realistic for the animals to spread word of the salt lick all over the globe? Why or why not? (*No. Animals can't talk.*)

PAGE 7 What activities described on this page suggest it is a fantasy? (*animals reading newspapers, knitting, mending, carrying coins*)

PAGE 9 What stores and places described on this page might you realistically expect to see in a town? (*laundry, market, book store, movie house, hot dog stand, school, and park*)

PAGE 12 What happens to the salt lick? (*The animals lick off all the salt.*)

PAGE 14 From reading this page, can you tell what a ghost town is? (*Possible response: It's a sad and empty place that was once a town.*)

REVISIT THE BOOK

READER RESPONSE

1. Possible responses: The animals talk. The animals build a community with buildings, stores, and a roller coaster.
2. Possible response: The town grows very quickly around one attraction. When the attraction is all used up, the town is deserted.
3. Possible responses: liked/like; walked/walk; stopped/stop; rolled/roll; wanted/want; chased/chase; fetched/fetch; agreed/agree; happened/happen; licked/lick; sniffed/sniff; owned/own
   Checked words: liked, chased, agreed
4. Possible response: They could have rationed the salt lick. They could have made sure the town had other things that would make the animals want to stay even after the salt lick was gone.

EXTEND UNDERSTANDING Invite students to contrast the story's illustrations and the photograph on page 16. Have students discuss why the author chose each medium.

RESPONSE OPTIONS

WRITING Ask students to pretend they are animals and to write about life in the salt lick town. They should describe why they came, what their friends and family are like, and what they do during the day.

WORD WORK Write a speak-aloud class story. It can be either a realistic story or a fantasy. First, write the vocabulary words on the board. Then start the story by saying a sentence that uses a word. Have students add on to the story, one at a time, each using a word on the list. Continue the story until all students have had a turn. Make sure the story has a conclusion.

SOCIAL STUDIES CONNECTION

Have students use the library or the Internet to research real ghost towns or boom towns. Have volunteers tell about their chosen towns and why they boomed.

Skill Work

TEACH/REVIEW VOCABULARY

Read aloud the vocabulary words. Ask students about words they may already know and explain words that are not familiar. Ask students what other meanings they might think of for the words *pick* and *boom*.

TARGET SKILL AND STRATEGY

REALISM AND FANTASY Tell students that a *realistic story* tells about something that could happen while a *fantasy* is a story about something that could not happen. Have students point out specific elements in the illustrations for *Salt Lick Boom Town* that indicate what type of story it is. Ask students to think of examples of realistic stories they have recently read. Then ask them to share examples of fantasies.

PRIOR KNOWLEDGE Tell students that *prior knowledge* is what they know about a given topic and is gathered from their reading and personal experiences. Explain how connecting prior knowledge to text can help students understand what they read. Look at the illustrations on pages 8 and 10–11. Ask students whether these illustrations remind them of anything familiar. Also help students understand that they can use their prior knowledge to determine whether a story is realism or fantasy. Ask: Have you ever seen a turtle standing in slippers walking with a cane? Invite students to point out how previously read books and their own life experiences suggest what type of story is told in *Salt Lick Boom Town*.

ADDITIONAL SKILL INSTRUCTION

THEME Tell students that as they read, they should think about the *theme*, or big idea, of the story. After students have finished reading, encourage them to state the theme. Ask: When you read this story, what did you learn about how communities form and why they might go away?

Realism and Fantasy

- A **realistic story** tells about something that could happen.
- A **fantasy** is a story about something that could not happen.

Directions Read the following passage. Then answer the questions below.

A boom town grew around the salt lick. Animals spent their days there. They brought their newspapers to the salt lick. Some animals brought their knitting and mending. The animals also brought coins. A clever raccoon built a store beside the salt lick. She sold ribbons and skillets and ladders and picks. She also sold cold drinks. Soon the salt lick had a book store, a movie house, and a hot dog stand. Animals built houses near the salt lick. They also built a school and a park.

1. Is this paragraph a realistic story or a fantasy?

_____

2. What is the first thing in the paragraph that makes you know what kind of story it is?

_____

_____

3. Why is it not realistic to say that animals brought knitting and mending to the salt lick?

_____

_____

4. What fantasy activity does the raccoon complete?

_____

5. When would it be realistic to have a boom town with a book store and a movie house?

_____

_____

Name _____

Vocabulary

Directions Choose the word from the box that best completes each sentence.
Write the word on the line. Two words are used more than once.

> ## Check the Words You Know
>
> ___ boom   ___ coins
> ___ fetched   ___ laundry
> ___ mending   ___ pick
> ___ skillet   ___ spell

1. Mom fried up the hamburgers in a _____ .

2. At the _____ , the children washed and dried their clothes.

3. At the store, the lady was _____ the torn clothes.

4. To play the card game, everyone needed to _____ a group of cards.

5. The children _____ the tools they needed to build the store.

6. Johnny wanted to pay for his book using _____ , not dollar bills.

7. The town was so quiet at night, it seemed a witch cast a _____ over it.

8. So many animals came to the salt lick that soon a _____ town grew.

9. If you want to learn to _____ well, try to read more.

10. The store sold the boy a _____ so he could break up the ice.

Directions Select three vocabulary words and write a sentence using each one.

11. _____

_____

12. _____

_____

13. _____

_____

Let's Make a Trade!

SUMMARY This book explains the benefits and the fun of bartering as an alternative to using money. It gives a brief history of how bartering began and how coins and paper money came into use. The book encourages students to try bartering.

LESSON VOCABULARY

carpenter	carpetmaker
knowledge	marketplace
merchant	plenty
straying	thread

INTRODUCE THE BOOK

INTRODUCE THE TITLE AND AUTHOR Discuss with students the title and the author of *Let's Make a Trade!* Based on the title and the cover illustration, ask students to describe what they imagine this book will be about.

BUILD BACKGROUND Ask: Have you ever traded something of yours for something that belonged to someone else? That's bartering. Discuss what other kinds of bartering students may have done and how they decided what something might be worth.

PREVIEW/USE TEXT FEATURES Have students look at the illustrations and read the captions. Suggest that students consider what extra information these elements provide about bartering.

READ THE BOOK

SET PURPOSE Have students set a purpose for reading *Let's Make a Trade!* Students' interest in acquiring new things without using money may guide this purpose. They might also be interested in the history of bartering. Suggest that students think about how goods can be obtained through trade instead of with money.

STRATEGY SUPPORT: SUMMARIZE As students read about bartering, prompt them to identify and write down the most important idea from each page. After reading, direct them to write a summary paragraph, using their notes as a guide. Invite volunteers to share their summaries with the class.

COMPREHENSION QUESTIONS

PAGES 8–9 What other things besides goods can be bartered? *(knowledge and skill)*

PAGE 9 What is a bartering plan? *(a list that details what skills or items you have to offer and what skills or items you need)*

PAGES 10–11 How did bartering help the radio station? *(The radio station got office space in exchange for running free ads.)*

PAGES 12–13 After reading about the sequence of events during "Bartering Day," what do you think the sequence of events for any trade should be? *(One person selects an item he or she no longer wants or needs. He or she displays the item for trade, and another person looks at it. Both traders can barter, bargain, trade, or decide to keep their item.)*

REVISIT THE BOOK

READER RESPONSE

1. Possible responses: Students brought items from home; students displayed their items; students looked at items for thirty minutes; some students bartered.

2. The theater gave the radio station its unused office space, and the radio station gave the theater free advertising in return.

3. *stray*; Possible sentence: Don't let the puppy stray too far.

4. Possible responses: One dad could barter his knowledge of how to start a small business. The other dad could barter his ability to do carpentry.

EXTEND UNDERSTANDING Suggest that students look at the diagram on pages 8–9. Diagrams are visual aids that can help you better understand the text. As students look at the diagram, ask them to discuss how the pictures help them understand what is being bartered. Draw students' attention to the arrows on pages 8–9 and ask how these arrows explain bartering more clearly.

RESPONSE OPTIONS

WRITING Have students write scripts for commercials that advertise something they are willing to barter. Invite students to perform their commercials for the class.

SOCIAL STUDIES CONNECTION

Have students make a bartering bulletin board. Decide with students ten classroom privileges, such as watering the plants, delivering messages, and holding the door. Have volunteers draw a picture of each privilege, and label and post it on the board. Next give each student three strips of colored paper. Students write on the strips what services they will exchange for the classroom privileges they would like. Then students thumbtack their strips to the privileges they want. Decide if you will accept each student strip in exchange for the privilege. When the barter is complete, have students take their strips off the board.

Skill Work

TEACH/REVIEW VOCABULARY

To reinforce the meaning of vocabulary words, make up a simple crossword puzzle with clues for students to fill out. Invite students to make up their own simple crossword puzzles for other students to complete. Post the completed crossword puzzles on the bulletin board.

ELL To help students gain familiarity with vocabulary, have them write simple riddles for each vocabulary word. Encourage students to share their riddles with each other.

TARGET SKILL AND STRATEGY

SEQUENCE Remind students that *sequence* is the order in which events occur. Ask students to make diagrams of the sequence of events for getting ready for and going to school, starting with "I wake up" and ending with "I enter my classroom." Invite students to illustrate each stage of their diagrams.

SUMMARIZE Remind students that *summarizing* means briefly retelling the key points of a story or of a series of events. Ask students to summarize a story they have recently read or a movie or TV program they have recently seen.

ADDITIONAL SKILL INSTRUCTION

DRAW CONCLUSIONS Remind students that *drawing conclusions* means thinking about facts and details and deciding something about them. Before students read the book, ask them to skim the pages and look at the examples of bartering through time. Ask students if they can draw any conclusions about the benefits of bartering, given that the ancient system of bartering still goes on today.

Sequence

- The **sequence** of events in a story is the order in which the events occur.

1. What is the sequence of events that goes on in bartering?

_____

_____

2. Describe the bartering that took place between the American colonists and Native Americans.

_____

_____

3. Describe the sequence of events in "Bartering Day" at school.

_____

_____

4. Trace the steps the community theater took to advertise its summer play.

_____

_____

5. Look at the bartering plan on pages 8 and 9. Write down a sequence of events for how the Smith family might barter with the Jones family.

_____

_____

_____

Vocabulary

Directions Unscramble each vocabulary word. Then write it on the line provided.

Check the Words You Know

___carpenter	___carpetmaker	___knowledge	___marketplace
___merchant	___plenty	___straying	___thread

1. acrpenter _____

2. gdnkowlee _____

3. ketplmarace _____

4. tylpen _____

5. ingtsray _____

6. readth _____

7. erpetcarmak _____

8. chantmer _____

Directions Complete each sentence with a word from the box.

9. The _____ is full of people buying and selling goods.

10. We have _____ of apples to bake a pie.

11. My mom used _____ to stitch the hole.

12. The skilled _____ tried to persuade me to buy one of his pictures.

Directions Write the definition of each vocabulary word below.

13. carpenter _____

_____

14. straying _____

_____

15. carpetmaker _____

_____

16. knowledge _____

_____

Let's Save Money!

SUMMARY Using characters as examples, this nonfiction book explains the basic steps in saving money and describes how bank savings accounts work. It covers topics such as opening savings accounts, earning interest, and creating savings plans.

LESSON VOCABULARY

college	dimes
downtown	fined
nickels	quarters
rich	

INTRODUCE THE BOOK

INTRODUCE THE TITLE AND AUTHOR Discuss with students the title and the author of *Let's Save Money!* Using the title, the cover illustration, and the genre as guides, have students suggest the topic of the book.

BUILD BACKGROUND Discuss with students their own experiences with saving money. Have volunteers describe why and how they saved it.

PREVIEW/USE TEXT FEATURES Have students look through the pictures. Draw their attention to those on pages 6–11, particularly the graphic on page 7. Ask: Are there any words or objects in these pictures that are unfamiliar to you? (*Possible responses: the word* interest, *the pictures of the savings books*) Discuss with students what they expect to learn from the book.

ELL Have students look closely at the picture of the bank on page 9. If students are unfamiliar with the concept of banks, have other English-speaking students explain how a bank works.

READ THE BOOK

SET PURPOSE Help students set their own purposes for reading the book by reviewing the unfamiliar illustrations they mentioned during the Preview section of the lesson. Suggest that students read to find out about those unfamiliar items.

STRATEGY SUPPORT: VISUALIZE To support students' visualizations of the text, have students write down the page numbers as they read whenever they find themselves visualizing information in the story. After students have finished reading, go back to the pages they noted and discuss how visualizing helped them understand the text.

COMPREHENSION QUESTIONS

PAGES 4–5 What is the author's purpose in describing how Kyle saved more money than Megan? (*Possible response: It gives the author a reason to explain how to save money in a bank.*)

PAGE 7 Visualize $8,144 in one-dollar bills. How big is the pile of money? (*Possible responses: as tall as I am; as big as my bed*)

PAGE 9 Why will Megan have more than $100 in her savings account by June if she sticks to her plan? (*The money in her savings account will earn interest.*)

PAGE 12 What sequence of events does Kyle follow each week with his five dollars? (*First, he puts two dollars into his college savings account; next, he donates a dollar to a food bank; then he keeps two dollars to spend for himself.*)

REVISIT THE BOOK

READER RESPONSE

1. Kyle receives five dollars each week. He puts two dollars into savings. He puts one dollar into the food bank. He keeps two dollars to spend.
2. Possible response: I saw myself at baseball camp.
3. Nickels, dimes, and quarters are all United States coins. Sentences will vary.
4. $6,381.41; $8,144.47

EXTEND UNDERSTANDING Point out that sometimes authors use graphic sources like time lines, graphs, or maps to help the reader understand information in the text. Have students look again at the graph on page 7. Discuss how the graph adds to their understanding of the text.

RESPONSE OPTIONS

WRITING Have students visualize savings goals for themselves. Have them write paragraphs describing their goals and imaginary savings plans that would allow them to save enough money to reach their goals.

MATHEMATICS CONNECTION

Divide the class into three or more teams. Have each team write math questions related to saving money on index cards, with the answers on the backs of the cards. Use the cards to play a math quiz game and keep team scores.

Skill Work

TEACH/REVIEW VOCABULARY

Read through the Glossary with students. To help them relate the vocabulary to the selection, have students create sentences that use both a vocabulary word and the word *money*. Provide the following example: *I want to save money to go to college.*

TARGET SKILL AND STRATEGY

SEQUENCE Review with students that *sequence* is the order in which events happen in a story or selection. Remind students that sometimes an author uses clue words such as *first*, *second*, *then*, *next*, *finally*, and *last* to show sequence, but sometimes the author may not. Have students look for sequence clue words as they read.

VISUALIZE Remind students that when they *visualize*, they make mental pictures of the people, events, and information in a text. Tell students that visualizing can help them better understand the story and follow the sequence of events. Suggest that students try to visualize events whenever they need to make sense of text.

ADDITIONAL SKILL INSTRUCTION

AUTHOR'S PURPOSE Remind students that authors always have a *purpose,* or reason, for writing: to inform, to persuade, to entertain, or to express a mood or feeling. Point out that authors often write with more than one purpose. Based on the genre and title of the book, ask: What do you think was the author's main purpose for writing? *(to inform the reader about how to save money)* Challenge students to find at least one other purpose the author may have had for writing the selection.

Sequence

- **Sequence** is the order in which things happen in a story or selection—what happens first, next, and last.

Directions Read the following passage. Answer each question below.

Darla wanted to go on the school trip to the beach. Darla decided she also wanted to buy a new bathing suit. She needed to save some money, and fast!

Darla decided to make a savings plan. First, she set a goal. She figured out how much money she wanted to save. She thought that $50 would cover everything.

She knew that the trip was in two months. Darla earned about ten dollars a week from her allowance and babysitting. She planned to save seven dollars a week. That would give her enough money for the trip. Finally, Darla went to the bank. She opened a savings account there. Her money would earn interest while it was in the bank.

1–3. How did Darla make her savings plan? Use sequence clue words to show the steps.

_____

_____

_____

_____

_____

4–6. What is the sequence of events in the passage? Use clue words to show the order.

_____

_____

_____

_____

_____

_____

© Pearson Education 3

Name _____

Vocabulary

Directions Choose the word from the box that best completes each sentence. Write the word on the line.

> ## Check the Words You Know
>
> ___college   ___dimes   ___downtown   ___fined
> ___nickels   ___quarters   ___rich

1. There are many businesses _____, so the city is often crowded during the workday.

2. I didn't have a dollar bill for the bus fare, so I gave the driver four

   _____.

3. Students who dream of going to _____ need to plan ahead by studying hard in school.

4. The police officer _____ the driver for leaving the car in a no-parking area.

5. A person with a lot of money may be _____, but that does not mean he is happy.

Directions Circle the word or words in each group that do NOT belong.

6. forks, spoons, dimes, knives

7. north, downtown, south, east

8. quarters, dimes, nickels, dollar bills

9. punished, jailed, fined, rewarded

10. summer camp, elementary school, college, high school

Directions Write a short paragraph about saving money. Use as many vocabulary words as you can.

_____

_____

Earning Money My Own Way

SUMMARY Andy finds a way to earn money to buy his share of a ticket to see his favorite band. He helps a neighbor, earns money doing something he enjoys, and meets his financial goal. The story helps support the lesson concept of how money can be earned, saved, and invested.

LESSON VOCABULARY

amount	check	earn
expensive	interest	million
thousand	value	worth

INTRODUCE THE BOOK

INTRODUCE THE TITLE AND AUTHOR Discuss with students the title and the author of *Earning Money My Own Way*. Based on the title and the illustration on the cover, ask students to describe whether they think this is a realistic story or a fantasy.

BUILD BACKGROUND Ask students to think of something that they would like to buy. Discuss jobs they would like to do to earn the money they would need. Ask: Does enjoying your work make it harder or easier?

PREVIEW/USE TEXT FEATURES As students preview the book, ask them how pictures can give clues to the meaning of the story. Ask: Who is the most important character in this story? How do you know? Discuss with students what thought balloons are and have students look at the thought balloons in the story. Ask how these balloons help tell the story. Point out the heading for the background information on page 16. Ask: Is this part of the story? Where in the book did the story end? What is the purpose of this part of the book?

READ THE BOOK

SET PURPOSE Have students set a purpose for reading *Earning Money My Own Way*. Students' interest in making decisions for themselves as well as earning money should propel this purpose. You may want to have them set a purpose immediately after their preview.

STRATEGY SUPPORT: MONITOR AND FIX UP Discuss with students that it is important to *monitor,* or keep an eye on, their understanding of what they are reading. Remind them that there are different ways to *fix up* a comprehension problem. Suggest that students write notes about what is happening in the story. Then they can track the story and can check their notes if the story stops making sense. Also tell students that if they are asked a question about the story, they can reread to review information they may have forgotten.

ELL Ask students to note words they don't understand. Suggest that they look the word up in a dictionary, write the meaning in their notebooks, and reread the part of the story where the word was used to check their understanding.

COMPREHENSION QUESTIONS

PAGE 4 Are the ways Andy thought of to get money realistic? Why or why not? (*They are realistic, because all three ways could happen.*)

PAGE 7 Why is babysitting not a good choice for Andy? (*Andy does not like babysitting.*)

PAGES 14–15 What work does Andy do for Mr. Thornton? Reread to find out. (*He pulls weeds, mows and waters the lawn, and collects the mail.*)

REVISIT THE BOOK

READER RESPONSE

1. Possible response: Yes, Andy could earn the money for half the ticket price.
2. Borrowing money would not work. Gift money would not work. Earning money was the answer.
3. Page 8: *Interest* is a feeling of wanting to know, see, do, or take part in something. Page 13: the money paid for the use of someone else's money
4. Possible response: I would do more chores around the house to get more allowance, because I like to help my parents.

EXTEND UNDERSTANDING Remind students that *setting* is the time and place of a story. Suggest that students go through the story and write down details in the text and art that show where and when this story takes place. Ask: Where does the story take place? When does the story take place? Would Andy be thinking of going to a concert if the setting were summer camp? What work might Andy do for Mr. Thornton if the story took place during a snowy winter?

RESPONSE OPTIONS

WORD WORK Discuss with students their reactions to words in the story that were used to exaggerate, such as *million* and *thousand*. Discuss why the author used those words on pages 9 and 12. Explain that large numbers, like *hundred* and *billion*, and undefined numbers, like *zillion*, are often used to exaggerate. Invite students to use number words to write exaggerated sentences. Have students share their sentences with the class.

SOCIAL STUDIES CONNECTION

To help students learn more about earning money, have them do different classroom chores. Use play money or counters as their earnings. You might also set up a simple banking system, so that students have a place to keep their money and a way to keep track of it.

Skill Work

TEACH/REVIEW VOCABULARY

Invite students to make a word web for each vocabulary word. Then have them supply at least two words that they associate with each vocabulary word.

TARGET SKILL AND STRATEGY

REALISM AND FANTASY Remind students that a *realistic story* tells about something that could happen, while a *fantasy* is a story about something that could not happen. On the board, write: *His sister grew wings. The boy mowed the grass.* Ask: I made up both of these sentences. Which one is realistic? Which is a fantasy? Why?

MONITOR AND FIX UP Remind students to *monitor* their understanding as they read. Tell them there are things they can do to *fix up* any comprehension problems they have. For example, they can take notes to keep track of what happens in a story or reread to locate information they may have forgotten. Remind students that if they have a good understanding of a story, it will be easier for them to tell if the story is a realistic story or a fantasy.

ADDITIONAL SKILL INSTRUCTION

CHARACTER Remind students that *characters* are the people or animals in stories. Tell them that sometimes authors do not tell everything about their characters. Students can also learn about characters from the characters' words and actions. Explain that students can use these clues to predict what a character will do next. Have students read the text on page 5. Ask: What do Andy's thoughts tell you about Andy? Students should see that Andy is willing to work for money. Then have students read page 13. Ask: Do you think that Andy will do the work, or will he goof off? Why?

Realism and Fantasy

- A **realistic story** tells about something that could happen.
- A **fantasy** is a story about something that could not happen.

Directions Write an *R* next to each statement that is realistic and an *F* next to each statement that is fantasy.

1. The brave mouse tamed the mighty lion. _____

2. Andy went with his parents to the movies. _____

3. The horse loved to read to the chickens. _____

4. She was as pretty as a movie star. _____

5. The sound of thunder is giants bowling in the sky. _____

6. Is *Earning Money My Own Way* a realistic story or a fantasy?

   _____

Directions Write four details from the book that support your answer to question 6.

7. _____

8. _____

9. _____

10. _____

Directions Write two statements about saving money that are fantasy.

11. _____

    _____

12. _____

    _____

Name _____

Vocabulary

Directions Read each clue. Write the word from the box that goes best with the clue. You may use a word more than once.

Check the Words You Know

___amount	___check	___earn
___expensive	___interest	___million
___thousand	___value	___worth

1. It is the number of things. _____

2. It is money you earn on money you save. _____

3. This means the worth of things. _____

4. This equals one and six zeros. _____

5. You might get paid with this. _____

6. Something that is this costs a lot of money. _____

7. This means to get something for doing something. _____

8. This equals ten hundreds. _____

9. You judge this when you decide the value of something. _____

10. You do this to make sure your shoes are tied. _____

Directions Write a sentence using as many vocabulary words as you can. Make sure the sentence makes sense.

_____

_____

_____

One Chili Pepper

SUMMARY This is a fictional story about a family who has moved to Mexico from the United States. It gives students information about different settings and shows how characters might act in a new setting.

LESSON VOCABULARY

arranged	bundles
dangerously	errands
excitedly	steady
unwrapped	wobbled

INTRODUCE THE BOOK

INTRODUCE THE TITLE AND AUTHOR Discuss with students the title and the author of the book *One Chili Pepper*. Direct students' attention to the cover illustration and ask them what the illustration makes them imagine the story might be about.

BUILD BACKGROUND Discuss if students have ever lived in a different culture, have visited a new place, or have tried new foods. Ask: How did that make you feel? Discuss with students if they have ever read any books about different countries and what they might have learned.

ELL Ask students to share their experiences of coming to a new culture. Discuss American food items that were new to them.

PREVIEW/USE ILLUSTRATIONS Invite students to look at the illustrations throughout the book and ask what information about the story these illustrations give them. Point out the expressions on the characters' faces, and ask students how this helps them understand what might be going on in the story.

READ THE BOOK

SET PURPOSE Have students set a purpose for reading *One Chili Pepper*. Their curiosity about living in a strange land and buying exotic vegetables should help guide this purpose.

STRATEGY SUPPORT: STORY STRUCTURE Suggest that students make a story map, labeled *Beginning, Middle,* and *End,* and have them fill in story details for each section. Discuss with students how the story would be changed if any of the events were put into a different order.

COMPREHENSION QUESTIONS

PAGE 3 What is the first problem of the story, and what is the plan to solve it? *(Dad needs a chili pepper, and Amelia goes out into the new neighborhood to get one.)*

PAGES 6–7 Use the illustrations to describe the setting of the open-air market. *(The streets are colorful, and there are vendors everywhere.)*

PAGE 14 What words would you use to describe Amelia? *(Possible responses: curious; adventuresome; excited)*

REVIST THE BOOK

READER RESPONSE

1. The setting is an open air market in Mexico.
2. Pots and pans wobble on a stand; a man buys a sombrero; Amelia buys a chili pepper.
3. Possible responses: standing, chopping, living, seeing, walking, selling, going, doing, talking, shopping. Sentences will vary.
4. Possible response: I would like to go to the Carribean to study the Taino culture. I like Taino music.

EXTEND UNDERSTANDING Remind students that *dialogue,* or speech, is what characters say to each other. Suggest that students look at the dialogue on page 15 when Amelia says, "Our shopping has been a great success." Discuss why Amelia says that and what it shows about her character.

RESPONSE OPTIONS

WRITING Suggest that students imagine they are Amelia and are writing letters home to the United States about their first weeks in Mexico. Have volunteers read their letters to the class.

SOCIAL STUDIES CONNECTION

Suggest that students research another country and its food. Then invite students to write a short story about going to a market to buy that food.

Skill Work

VOCABULARY

Review vocabulary words with students. Provide sentences in which the vocabulary words have been used incorrectly, and ask students to correct the sentences.

TARGET SKILL AND STRATEGY

CHARACTER AND SETTING Remind students that the *character* is the person or animal who is doing the action of the story, and the *setting* is the time and place of the story. Explain that what a person does can show what kind of person he or she is. For example, if someone feeds a stray cat, we can imagine that person is kind. Encourage students to record details that show what Amelia is like. Remind students that the setting can also influence how a character acts and that, as they read, they should make notes about the setting and about how the character acts in it.

STORY STRUCTURE Remind students that stories are arranged in a sequence with a beginning, a middle, and an end. Discuss how stories usually have a problem that must be solved before the end. Suggest that as students read, they map out the *story structure*, writing down what the problem is, how it is being solved, and what happens at the end of the story. Remind students that understanding the story structure can also help them understand the characters and the setting.

ADDITIONAL SKILL INSTRUCTION

GENERALIZE Remind students that a *generalization* is a broad statement that applies to many examples. Clue words like *everyone, always, in general,* and *none* can help students identify generalizations. Remind students that not all generalizations are true, especially if there are no facts to support them; for example: All classical music is played loudly. Then suggest that students make generalizations about what they read.

Name _____

Character and Setting

- **Character** is the person or animal who does the action in the story.
- The **setting** is the time and place of the story.

Directions What kind of person is Amelia in the story *One Chili Pepper*?
Read the details below, and then tell how those details describe what kind of
person Amelia is.

1. Amelia offers to go shop for a chili pepper in a strange neighborhood. This shows

_____.

2. Amelia decides to buy the chili pepper at the open-air market instead of going to a
   regular store. This shows she is

_____.

3. Amelia watches someone bargaining with a vendor. When it's her turn to buy the
   chili, she bargains too. This shows she is

_____.

4. How would you act in an open-air market? Imagine you are in the open-air
   market setting and are looking to bargain for something. What food
   would you want to buy and why? How much would you bargain?
   Write a short paragraph about your experience.

_____

_____

_____

_____

_____

_____

_____

Vocabulary

Directions Find the misspelled vocabulary word or words in each sentence and correct them. Then write a sentence of your own using the same vocabulary words.

Check the Words You Know

___arranged   ___bundles   ___dangerously   ___errands
___excitedly   ___steady   ___unwrapped   ___wobbled

1. Amelia completed all of her erands at the market and unrapped her packages

   when she got home. _____ _____

   _____

   _____

2. "I love chili peppers!" said Ben excitly. _____

   _____

   _____

3. The salesperson sorted the fruit neatly into big bundels. _____

   _____

   _____

4. The pile of pots and pans was not stedy and wobbled dangresly.

   _____ _____

   _____

   _____

Directions Write a short paragraph about a character you make up. Use as many vocabulary words as you can.

_____

_____

_____

_____

Birds That Can't Fly!

SUMMARY Birds that cannot fly can still thrive in different environments. This book introduces the reader to flightless birds from around the world. It explains how key characteristics help the emu, flightless cormorant, and others meet their survival needs.

LESSON VOCABULARY

cuddles	flippers
frozen	hatch
pecks	preen
snuggles	

INTRODUCE THE BOOK

INTRODUCE THE TITLE AND AUTHOR Discuss with students the title and the author of *Birds That Can't Fly!* Ask: What can you learn about flightless birds by looking at the cover photograph? Talk about what information students think the author will provide based on the title and cover.

BUILD BACKGROUND Have students think about birds with which they are familiar. Ask students where they have seen birds—including outdoors, TV, and the zoo. Discuss what students have noticed about birds. Ask students if they think there are skills other than flying that can help birds move and survive.

PREVIEW/USE TEXT FEATURES Point out that the photographs on pages 3, 5, and 14 are paired together for specific reasons. Ask students how pairing the photos helps illustrate important ideas on each page.

READ THE BOOK

SET PURPOSE Have students set a purpose for reading *Birds That Can't Fly!* This purpose should be guided by the impressions they get from skimming the photos, captions, and maps, along with their own curiosity.

STRATEGY SUPPORT: GRAPHIC ORGANIZERS Tell students that different graphic organizers are suited for different purposes. Webs and charts, for example, can help readers determine cause and effect, compare and contrast story elements, and track vocabulary. Introduce readers to organizers for a variety of purposes, and encourage their use during reading.

COMPREHENSION QUESTIONS

PAGE 3 Contrast flightless birds with flying birds. (*Flightless birds have heavier bones and their feathers are different from those of flying birds.*)

PAGES 5–6 How are ostriches and emus alike and different? (*Both ostriches and emus eat plants. Ostriches live in Africa, and emus live in Australia.*)

PAGES 6, 11 How do birds such as emus and flightless cormorants meet their needs without the ability to fly? (*Emus have powerful legs, and flightless cormorants can swim well. This allows them to move quickly and survive.*)

PAGES 8–9 What does the map tell you about flightless birds? (*Different varieties live all over the world.*)

REVISIT THE BOOK

READER RESPONSE

1. Possible response: There are many different kinds of flightless birds.
2. In descending order of weight: Male ostrich: 300 pounds; Cassowary: 130 pounds; Flightless cormorant: 9 pounds
3. Possible responses: He climbed through the ship's *hatch* to get on deck. He decided to *hatch* a plan to get the money.
4. the flightless cormorant of the Galápagos Islands

EXTEND UNDERSTANDING Have students look at the map on pages 8–9. Discuss how the call-outs draw attention to specific species of flightless birds and where they live. Then ask how the call-outs would change if the map focused entirely on flying birds and their habitats. What would the call-outs show and where would they point? Students may use reference sources to gather information on flying birds.

RESPONSE OPTIONS

WRITING Ask: If you could be any flightless bird, which one would you be and why? Have students answer in one or two paragraphs.

ELL Invite students to draw a picture of a flightless bird and write bilingual labels or captions for its body parts.

WORD WORK Challenge students to write or verbalize sentences that incorporate two or more vocabulary words. Provide an example, such as, *The penguin chick snuggles and cuddles with its mother to stay warm.*

SCIENCE CONNECTION

Invite students to use reference sources to learn more about what characteristics help flightless birds thrive.

Skill Work

TEACH/REVIEW VOCABULARY

Have volunteers demonstrate their knowledge of vocabulary words by acting them out and/or incorporating them into sentences.

TARGET SKILL AND STRATEGY

MAIN IDEA Tell students that the *main idea* is the most important idea about the topic. To find it, students must determine the relative importance of information they read. *Supporting details* are pieces of information that tell more about the main idea. Model how to ask questions to find the main idea of a book. Ask: In a word or two, what is this book about? (This identifies the topic.) What is the most important idea about the topic? (This identifies the main idea.) What are some details that tell more about the main idea? As students read, have them think about the main idea.

GRAPHIC ORGANIZERS *Graphic organizers* are pictorial devices that help students view and construct relationships among concepts. For example, they can use a graphic organizer to help them identify the main idea and supporting details of a passage. Before students read, create a *KWL* (*K*now, *W*ant to know, *L*earned) chart on the board about flightless birds. Ask students to share what they already know about these birds and to identify what they would like to know about them. During reading, have students look for answers to their questions and tell what they have learned about flightless birds. Record responses in the chart.

ADDITIONAL SKILL INSTRUCTION

COMPARE AND CONTRAST Tell students that to *compare* is to identify how two or more things are alike, whereas to *contrast* is to identify how they are different. Ask students to compare and contrast aspects of flightless birds in the book, such as their natural habitats. Suggest that students use a chart to keep track of similarities and differences.

Main Idea

- The **main idea** is the most important idea about a paragraph, passage, or story.
- **Details** are pieces of information that tell more about the main idea.

Directions Read the following passage. Then answer the questions below.

Birds that cannot fly are called flightless birds. They differ from flying birds in many ways. The bones of flightless birds are heavier than those of flying birds. Flightless birds' feathers are also different from those of flying birds. Like humans, all birds have a breastbone. However, a flightless bird's breastbone is different from that of a flying bird since it has no flight muscles attached.

1. In one or two words, what is this paragraph about?

_____

2. What is the main idea of the paragraph?

_____

_____

3. What is one important detail that tells more about the main idea?

_____

_____

4. What is another important detail about the main idea?

_____

_____

5. What is a third detail about the main idea?

_____

_____

Name _____

Vocabulary

Directions Read each numbered vocabulary word and the four words that follow it.
Circle the two words that are synonyms for the vocabulary word.

Check the Words You Know

___cuddles   ___flippers   ___frozen   ___hatch
___pecks   ___preen   ___snuggles

1. cuddles

slaps   hugs   throws   snuggles

2. flippers

eyes   paddles   fins   noses

3. frozen

chilly   icy   melted   burned

4. hatch

fall   fly   produce   cause

5. pecks

strikes   walks   swims   hits

6. preen

see   dress   groom   laugh

7. snuggles

nestles   avoids   holds   kicks

Directions Write a paragraph about penguins using at least four vocabulary words.

_____

_____

_____

_____

35

The Boy Who Cried Wolf

SUMMARY In a retelling of the classic tale *The Boy Who Cried Wolf,* a bored young shepherd named Daniel enjoys getting attention by crying "wolf" even though there is no wolf threatening his sheep. But he learns an important lesson when a real wolf appears one day and the villagers ignore Daniel's cries.

LESSON VOCABULARY

excitement   gardener
motioned   sadness
shivered   shocked
slammed

INTRODUCE THE BOOK

INTRODUCE THE TITLE AND AUTHOR Discuss with students the title and the author of *The Boy Who Cried Wolf.* Point out that the cover states that it has been retold by the author. Ask: What is a retelling of a story? What types of stories are often retold?

BUILD BACKGROUND Have students discuss what it means to be responsible and trustworthy. Ask volunteers to share instances where someone had trust in them and why it was important to maintain that trust.

PREVIEW/USE TEXT FEATURES Ask students to preview the book by looking at the illustrations. Have them focus on the characters' poses and facial expressions, and ask what they can tell about the characters based on the pictures.

READ THE BOOK

SET PURPOSE Have students set a purpose for reading *The Boy Who Cried Wolf.* Suggest that they think about real-life experiences where they, like the boy mentioned in the title, were given big responsibilities. How did they try to fulfill these responsibilities? Did they look for an easy way out, or did they work hard? What did they learn from their experiences? Tell students they can ask these same questions about the boy in the story and seek answers while reading.

STRATEGY SUPPORT: VISUALIZE Reinforce students' recall of the book by asking them to close their eyes and form mental pictures of what the author described. They should then draw pictures of what they visualized and compare their drawings with the illustrations in the book.

COMPREHENSION QUESTIONS

PAGE 5 What did Daniel's actions tell you about his character? *(He was restless and mischievious.)*

PAGE 6 What did the villagers do when Daniel cried "wolf"? Why? *(They rushed up the hill. They were afraid a wolf would eat the sheep.)*

PAGE 12 Why did the villagers ignore Daniel's cries for help? *(They began ignoring him after he had tricked them twice.)*

PAGE 15 If you were the farmer, would you have trusted Daniel to work for you? Why or why not? *(Possible response: Yes. Everyone deserves a second chance.)*

REVISIT THE BOOK

READER RESPONSE

1. Responses will vary.
2. Possible response: The village might be a good place to live because it is peaceful and pretty. It might not be such a good place because there would not be many things to do there.
3. Possible response: *sadness*—unhappiness, *shivered*—shook, *shocked*—surprised, *slammed*—smashed, *motioned*—pointed.
4. Responses will vary.

EXTEND UNDERSTANDING Introduce students to the element of theme by asking questions such as, "What does the author want readers to learn from reading this story?" Have them determine the story's big idea and explain how the events and characters support their findings.

RESPONSE OPTIONS

WRITING Have students pretend they are either Daniel or the farmer. Ask those who are Daniel to write a letter to the farmer explaining how Daniel feels about him and what he plans to do as his worker. Those who are the farmer should write a letter to Daniel stating how the farmer feels about him and what he expects as his boss.

WORD WORK Point out that vocabulary words such as *gardener* and *sadness* are made up of base words and special endings called suffixes which can change the meanings of base words. For example, *farm* becomes *farmer* by adding the suffix *-er*. Ask volunteers to cite other examples.

SOCIAL STUDIES CONNECTION

Have students identify people with jobs based on trust, such as police officers. Invite one of them to talk to your class about why trust is an important part of his or her work.

Skill Work

TEACH/REVIEW VOCABULARY

Have volunteers help the rest of the class better understand the vocabulary words by defining them in their own words or using pantomime.

TARGET SKILL AND STRATEGY

CHARACTER Tell students that a *character* is a person who takes part in the events of a story. Ask them to identify the main characters in the book. Explain that the qualities or characteristics of a character are known as *character traits* and that these traits usually relate to personalities. While students are reading, have them identify clues and details that tell about the traits of specific characters. Ask them to predict what the characters will do next based on those traits.

ELL Ask students simple questions about the characters, plot, or theme.

VISUALIZE *Visualizing* is particularly useful when exploring characters in greater depth. To create memorable and meaningful mental pictures of characters, students should use their own experiences and knowledge when they visualize. Have them relate details of characters in the story to details of real people they can recall from their own experiences.

ADDITIONAL SKILL INSTRUCTION

DRAW CONCLUSIONS Explain that when you *draw a conclusion* you reach a decision after thinking about details in what you read. When students use details to make reasonable decisions about characters or events, they are drawing conclusions. Invite students to create a web or chart to write down facts that led them to a specific conclusion about the characters or events in the book.

Character

- A **character** is a person who takes part in the events of a story.
- The qualities of a character are known as **character traits** and usually tell about his or her personality.

Directions Follow the directions below to describe the boy who cried "Wolf!"

1. Name the main character.

_____

2. Write two sentences about Daniel's character traits.

_____

_____

_____

3. Write three sentences about what Daniel wants.

_____

_____

_____

_____

_____

Directions Write four sentences about what Daniel does and feels during the story.

4. _____

_____

5. _____

_____

6. _____

_____

7. _____

_____

Vocabulary

Directions Below each vocabulary word is a list of four words. Find two other words that have almost the same meaning as the vocabulary word. Circle them.

Check the Words You Know

| ___excitement | ___gardener | ___motioned | ___sadness |
| ___shivered | ___shocked | ___slammed | |

1. sadness

   unhappiness   sorrow   delight   joy

2. slammed

   smashed   petted   smacked   touched

3. shivered

   sat   trembled   shook   stood

4. excitement

   boredom   action   dullness   adventure

5. gardener

   grower   fisherman   shepherd   farmer

6. motioned

   fell   pointed   stared   signaled

7. shocked

   surprised   jolted   certain   confident

Directions What do you think happened after the story ended? Write a paragraph about how Daniel and the farmer worked together. Use as many vocabulary words as you can.

_____

_____

_____

Katy's Last-Minute Book Report

SUMMARY A girl named Katy puts off reading a book for an assigned book report. When she is forced to finish her book and write about it during one very stressful weekend, Katy vows to never again leave any assignment until the last minute.

LESSON VOCABULARY

collection	enormous
realize	scattered
shiny	strain

INTRODUCE THE BOOK

INTRODUCE THE TITLE AND AUTHOR Discuss with students the title and the author of *Katy's Last-Minute Book Report*. How does the cover illustration support the title? What situations might the author have in mind for Katy based on these elements?

BUILD BACKGROUND Have students discuss situations in which they put off assignments or tasks until the last minute. What challenges did they face while trying to meet their deadlines?

PREVIEW/USE TEXT FEATURES As students look through the illustrations, have them focus on the characters' poses and facial expressions. Then discuss what they think the characters are doing.

READ THE BOOK

SET PURPOSE Have students set a purpose for reading *Katy's Last-Minute Book Report*. This purpose may be guided by students' own experiences with completing school assignments at the last minute. Ask them to think about what they learned from these experiences and what Katy, the main character of the book, might learn from hers.

STRATEGY SUPPORT: MONITOR AND FIX UP Remind students that rereading and reviewing can help them answer their questions about text, find the main idea, and restore comprehension when their understanding breaks down. Tell students that seeking help from both teachers and peers can further boost their problem-solving skills. Encourage them to help each other and learn how to ask good questions by providing opportunities for cooperative work, reading circles, and so on.

COMPREHENSION QUESTIONS

PAGE 4 Katy's friend, Pam, began working on her book report early. How do you think Pam's report turned out? Why? *(Possible response: Pam's report probably turned out well because she gave herself enough time to finish it.)*

PAGES 6–10 What drew Katy's attention away from writing her report? In what order did these activities happen? *(Katy was first distracted by soccer practice, then by watching TV, then by working on a coin collection, the need to clean up her room, and a soccer game.)*

PAGE 15 What did Katy promise to do after she handed in her book report? Why? *(Katy promised to never leave anything until the last minute again because cramming for her book report was so stressful.)*

REVISIT THE BOOK

READER RESPONSE

1. Possible response: The longer Katy put off doing her report the more stressed she felt and the more fun things she had to pass up.

2. Katy missed watching a video, enjoying the soccer game, going out for ice cream, and going with Pam for pizza and a movie.

3. The base words are *inform* and *collect.* Possible sentences: When are you going to inform your teacher of your book selection? Chris decided to collect baseball cards.

4. Possible answer: Start my homework earlier.

EXTEND UNDERSTANDING Tell students that a *plot* is an organized pattern of events in a story. Use simple story maps with students to help them determine and note the most important events of the story. For example, point out that Katy's soccer game on page 10 is important because it is yet another obstacle that prevents Katy from writing her report on time, whereas the place where her teammates decide to have ice cream afterward is not important to the pattern of the story.

RESPONSE OPTIONS

WRITING Tell students that Katy might have had fewer problems if she had created and followed a timetable of things to do for her book report. Invite students to select a real-life assignment with a deadline and create a timetable of things they must do in order to meet the deadline.

WORD WORK Create sentences with each of the vocabulary words, but leave a blank space where each vocabulary word should be. Provide students with a word bank of vocabulary to complete the sentences.

SOCIAL STUDIES CONNECTION

Many people face deadlines as part of their daily routines. Discuss what kinds of jobs involve deadlines and why it is important for people with those jobs to manage their time carefully.

Skill Work

TEACH/REVIEW VOCABULARY

Ask students to find how each vocabulary word is used in the book. Encourage them to use the illustrations for clues to define the vocabulary in their own words.

TARGET SKILL AND STRATEGY

MAIN IDEA Explain to students that the *main idea* in fiction tells what the story is about and identifies its most important ideas. Ask students to identify important ideas and details while they are reading the book and then explain what it is about in their own words.

MONITOR AND FIX UP When students *monitor* comprehension, they know when they understand what they read and when they do not. Remind students of *fix-up* strategies, such as rereading and reviewing, that can restore their understanding when problems arise. Encourage students to use this strategy when their understanding of the text breaks down. They may also reread if they have a question after reading. Coach students and use teacher-directed questioning in small groups to reinforce the importance of rereading to find information. Tell them using this strategy to monitor comprehension on their own will help them find the main idea of the story.

ELL Ask students to identify words in the book that they are struggling with. Help them create a bilingual glossary based on these words.

ADDITIONAL SKILL INSTRUCTION

SEQUENCE Tell students that a story's *sequence* tells the order in which events occur. Using sequence skills to keep track of which events happened first, next, and last is essential for a correct understanding of books such as *Katy's Last-Minute Book Report*. Ask volunteers to explain how the events of the beginning and middle of the story have a dramatic effect on its ending.

Main Idea

- The **main idea** is the most important idea about a paragraph, passage, or story.
- **Details** are small pieces of information that tell more about the main idea.

Directions Read the following passage. Then answer the questions below.

Third-grade students have many things to do each day. Homework, sports, and family activities take up a lot of time.

It can be hard to decide what to do when. If you don't plan your time well, you might forget to do something important. Sometimes people put off doing things until the last minute. Then they don't have enough time left to do a good job.

1. Use one to three words to tell what this paragraph is about.

_____

_____

2. What is the main idea of the paragraph?

_____

_____

3. What is one detail that tells more about the main idea?

_____

_____

4. What is another detail about the main idea?

_____

_____

5. What is a third detail about the main idea?

_____

_____

© Pearson Education 3

Name _____

Vocabulary

Directions Read each numbered vocabulary word and the four words that follow it. Circle the two words that are synonyms for the vocabulary word.

Check the Words You Know

___collection	___enormous	___realize
___scattered	___shiny	___strain

1. collection

group   set   scattering   book

2. enormous

huge   tiny   medium   giant

3. realize

forget   overlook   recognize   understand

4. scattered

grouped   separated   sprinkled   sorted

5. shiny

glossy   dull   sparkly   cloudy

6. strain

achieve   try   strive   complete

Directions Write a paragraph that includes at least four of the vocabulary words.

_____

_____

_____

_____

_____

_____

Our Garden

SUMMARY This is a story about how a group of kids transforms an empty urban lot into a beautiful garden. They get the entire community involved, which brings both beauty and a fresh community spirit to the town.

LESSON VOCABULARY

bottom	cheat
clever	crops
lazy	partners
wealth	

INTRODUCE THE BOOK

INTRODUCE THE TITLE AND AUTHOR Discuss with students the title and the author of *Our Garden*. Based on the title, ask students to describe any images they may have about the story. Suggest students also look at the cover illustration. Ask: How does this picture relate to the title?

BUILD BACKGROUND Discuss with students what they know about planting. Ask them if they understand what is involved in growing plants. Discuss any projects students have done in groups, such as decorating the classroom for a holiday or preparing a group report, and whether it was easier to complete the project when everyone worked together.

ELL Invite students to share words from their home languages related to planting or gardens. Post these words on a bulletin board beside the English words.

PREVIEW/USE ILLUSTRATIONS As students preview the book, suggest that they notice how the artwork shows groups of people, rather than individuals. Discuss why students think the artist did this. Ask them to note the title of the story, *Our Garden,* and to discuss how it connects to the illustrations.

READ THE BOOK

SET PURPOSE Have students set a purpose for reading *Our Garden*. Students' interest in gardening or plants should guide this purpose. Suggest that students also consider how working together for a common good can help their own community.

STRATEGY SUPPORT: PREDICT As students read about the group working to transform the lot into a community garden, tell them that predicting can give them a chance to use what they already know to make connections with what will happen next. Predicting also allows them to make sense of the story and gives them a stake in the outcome. Encourage students to write their predictions and to check them against what happens in the story.

COMPREHENSION QUESTIONS

PAGE 4 Why would a garden give the old lot new life? *(Possible response: A garden is full of growing, living things.)*

PAGE 5 Why do you think Mayor Smith is so excited about the garden? *(Possible response: He knows the children's garden will benefit the whole community.)*

PAGE 9 How do the workers at City Hall help with the garden? *(They collect money and pay for the plants, seeds, and soil needed for the garden.)*

PAGE 15 What is the author's purpose in writing a story about a whole community getting involved in a project? *(Possible response: He wants to show how everyone has fun and benefits from working together.)*

REVISIT THE BOOK

READER RESPONSE

1. Possible response: to show how rundown the lot had become and how much work the kids needed to do
2. Possible response: People will see what a lovely spot the lot has become and will help take care of the garden.
3. Possible response: *crops* as a verb means "to shorten." Possible sentence: The haircutter *crops* five inches off the child's hair.
4. Possible response: don't litter, no loud music, no fighting, no dogs allowed in the garden

EXTEND UNDERSTANDING Remind students that the *setting* is the time and the place where a story takes place, and that the setting can affect what happens in the story and why. Discuss with students whether this particular story could have happened in any other time or place. If so, would it have had the same end results? Discuss with students how the story would be different if it had happened in a very small country village, for example, or in the year 2233.

RESPONSE OPTIONS

WORD WORK Discuss with students their reaction to the word *community*. In this story, the community is a town and its people. Ask students if they know any other kinds of communities or organizations. Make a diagram with students about the class community. The diagram should show who is in the community and how they work together for the common good of the whole classroom.

SCIENCE CONNECTION

Students can learn more about how plants grow by growing their own bean plants from seeds in the classroom. Suggest that students make a chart with assigned jobs for watering, tracking growth, cleaning up loose soil, and other gardening tasks. Post the chart in the classroom.

Skill Work

TEACH/REVIEW VOCABULARY

To reinforce the contextual meaning of the vocabulary words, ask students to write sentences using each word. Then invite students to build a *word wall* where they will come up with other words that have to do with plants. Suggest that students position these words on the wall so that they form a picture that resembles a growing plant with many leaves and branches.

TARGET SKILL AND STRATEGY

AUTHOR'S PURPOSE Remind students that every author writes a story for a *purpose,* or reason, such as to entertain, give information, persuade, or teach. Ask students why they think the author wrote this story. Suggest that as students read, they track and make note of any story details that might support their answers.

PREDICT Remind students that to *predict* means to guess what you think might happen next in a story based on what has already happened. Suggest that students pause once or twice while they read the story to make predictions about what is going to happen. Then they can see whether their predictions were right, as they continue to read.

ADDITIONAL SKILL INSTRUCTION

PLOT Remind students that *plot* is the series of events in a story. Instruct students that as they read, they should look for a problem or conflict that the story is posing. Then they can figure out what is happening in the beginning of the story, the middle of the story, and at the end of the story, when the conflict is resolved.

Author's Purpose

- The **author's purpose** is the reason or reasons the author has for writing.
- To *inform, persuade, entertain,* or *express* are common reasons for writing.

Directions Answer the questions.

1. Why do you think the author gave so many details about how everyone cleaned up the empty lot?

_____

_____

2. Why do you think the author wrote a book about a group of people building a garden rather than just one person?

_____

_____

3. Explain why one of the purposes the author may have had was to inform.

_____

_____

4. How did the author show she also wanted to entertain?

_____

_____

5. In what way did the author try to persuade?

_____

_____

Name _____

Vocabulary

Directions Find the vocabulary word that matches each clue below.

> ### Check the Words You Know
>
> ___bottom   ___cheat
> ___clever   ___crops
> ___lazy   ___partners
> ___wealth

1. It means a large amount of. _____

2. It means the opposite of hardworking. _____

3. It means the opposite of top. _____

4. If a contest was dishonest, you might say it was trying to do this to people. _____

5. We use this word to describe a person who likes to lie around all day. _____

6. We use this word to describe kinds of plants you grow to eat. _____

7. This word is used to describe someone who is smart. _____

8. If you and somebody else are these, you work together toward a goal. _____

Directions Write a sentence that uses two of the vocabulary words.

_____

_____

_____

_____

The Colonial Adventure

SUMMARY This fiction book recounts life in colonial New England from the perspectives of two young cousins, Elizabeth and Sarah. Elizabeth, whose family is just beginning to settle in Massachusetts, gets a preview of colonial life from her cousin, who writes letters about her family's earlier settlement in Virginia. Their stories reveal the challenges of colonial living and how it differed from the life they left behind in England.

LESSON VOCABULARY

barrels	cellar	clearing
peg	spoil	steep

INTRODUCE THE BOOK

INTRODUCE THE TITLE AND AUTHOR Discuss with students the title and the author of *The Colonial Adventure*. Ask them to look at the cover illustration and talk about how it might relate to the title. Who is the girl pictured? Where is she? What is she looking at?

BUILD BACKGROUND Point out the locations of England, Virginia, and Massachusetts on a large map. Ask students to discuss what traveling between these places must have been like in a time when only slower forms of transportation existed. Talk about how people's lives in these places may have differed as a result of their distances from each other.

PREVIEW/USE TEXT FEATURES Tell students to look at the sketches on pages 6, 7, and 12. Ask them how the labels on the sketches further their understanding of Elizabeth and Sarah's voyage from England as well as the cousins' experiences in the New World.

READ THE BOOK

SET PURPOSE Have students set a purpose for reading *The Colonial Adventure*. Read aloud the title and ask what the word *adventure* brings to mind. Tell students to look at the cover illustration and talk about how it hints at adventure. Their concepts of adventure should guide their purpose.

STRATEGY SUPPORT: ASK QUESTIONS On chart paper, create a four-column chart where the literary elements of setting, character, plot, and theme appear as column heads. Then invite students to ask questions about important information they gather in each of these categories while reading. Later on, have volunteers share any answers they find, along with any conclusions they have drawn as a result.

COMPREHENSION QUESTIONS

PAGES 4–5 How did Elizabeth travel to New England with her family? *(They sailed from England on board a crowded ship for two months.)*

PAGE 8 What did Elizabeth notice most about Massachusetts as her ship reached land? *(It was huge.)*

PAGE 11 Do you think Elizabeth's first winter in Massachusetts was a happy time? Why? *(No. There was not enough food to eat and colonists got sick.)*

PAGE 14 From whom did colonists get valuable advice on farming? *(New England's native peoples taught the colonists how to plant pumpkin, squash, and corn.)*

REVISIT THE BOOK

READER RESPONSE

1. The weather in Massachusetts was cold and its land was rocky, while the weather in Virginia was hot and its land was swampy. People in Massachusetts grew corn, and those in Virginia grew wheat and tobacco.

2. Responses will vary.

3. Possible responses: Food *spoils* if you leave it out. The mother *spoils* her son by giving him everything he wants. My sister *spoils* our card games by cheating.

4. Responses will vary.

EXTEND UNDERSTANDING Tell students that characters are the people who take part in the events of a story. Ask students to look for clues such as the characters' words and actions so they can explore the characters in greater depth.

RESPONSE OPTIONS

WRITING Invite students to write and act out a skit about life in colonial America from either Elizabeth's or Sarah's perspective.

WORD WORK Tell students that *synonyms* are words that have the same or nearly the same meaning. For example, *basement* is a synonym for the vocabulary word *cellar* and *rot* is a synonym for the word *spoil*.

ELL Look over the book's illustrations with students. Have them point to items they see and then name them in English and their home languages.

SOCIAL STUDIES CONNECTION

Many different kinds of people established England's Thirteen Colonies for a variety of reasons. Provide reference materials that will help students explore the colonists' diverse experiences. Then have them each choose a colony and write a letter from the perspective of someone living there.

Skill Work

TEACH/REVIEW VOCABULARY

Before reading, introduce the lesson vocabulary words by asking students if they recognize any of them. Have volunteers use the words in sentences based on real-life experiences to help others better understand the vocabulary.

TARGET SKILL AND STRATEGY

DRAW CONCLUSIONS A *conclusion* is a decision you reach after you think about details in what you have read. Ask students to use what they read plus common sense and past experiences to *draw conclusions* about Elizabeth and Sarah's lives. Suggest that they use a diagram such as a simple web to write facts that support a conclusion.

ASK QUESTIONS Remind students of the importance of *asking questions* about important text information. Tell students that good questions often start with *who, what, when, where, why,* or *how.* Good questions also ask about important details. Ask students to write down questions they have while reading about Elizabeth and Sarah's lives. The strategy of asking questions can help students draw conclusions by helping them construct meaning and integrate new information. Invite volunteers to share questions they asked and answered while reading. Then have them describe how questioning helped them draw conclusions.

ADDITIONAL SKILL INSTRUCTION

SETTING Tell students that the time and place of a story is its *setting.* Help them focus on words, phrases, and comparisons that are related to the book's setting by using questions, examples, and other prompts. Then ask them to describe how setting affected the main characters' actions and feelings.

Name _____

Draw Conclusions

- To **draw a conclusion** means to use what you already know and what you have read to make reasonable decisions about characters or events.

Directions Read the following message written by a fictional person from England who has settled in colonial Jamestown. Then fill in the charts with facts from the passage and things you know that are related to the facts. Finally, write conclusions based on the facts and what you know.

Sometimes life in New World can be difficult. The land here is very different from England. Jamestown is filled with swamps. Because the land is swampy, the water that we drink is brown, muddy, and not at all fresh. Also, the people of our settlement are trying to make friends with the native people. But there is little that they understand about us or that we understand about them. Papa says that we should still try to work with them and respect their ways.

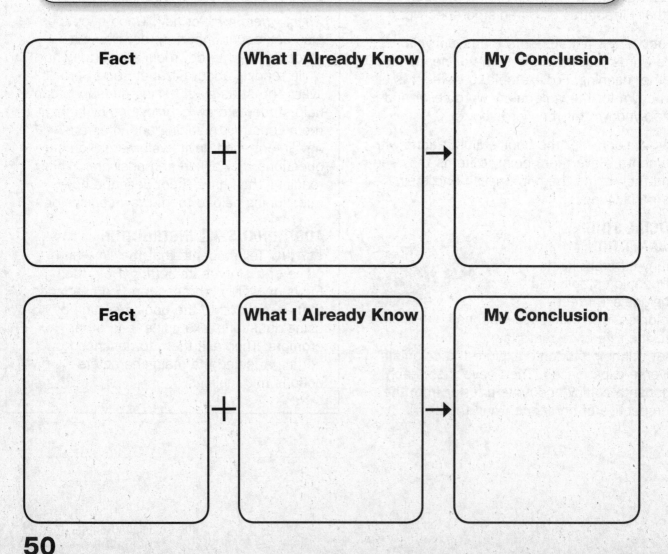

Vocabulary

Directions Read each list of words. Write a vocabulary word that relates to each group.

> ## Check the Words You Know
> ___barrels   ___cellar   ___clearing
> ___peg   ___spoil   ___steep

1. _____

    hanger

    hook

    rod

2. _____

    sharp

    sudden

    raised

3. _____

    ruin

    rot

    decay

4. _____

    cans

    buckets

    containers

5. _____

    empty space

    gap

    opening

6. _____

    basement

    underground room

    vault

Directions Write a paragraph about life in colonial New England. Use as many vocabulary words as you can.

_____

_____

_____

_____

_____

Tulips for Annie's Mother

SUMMARY Like many people, Annie's family struggled during the Great Depression. This fictional book shows students how the Great Depression changed the country and the people living here.

LESSON VOCABULARY

beauty	blooming
bulbs	doze
humor	recognizing
showers	sprouting

INTRODUCE THE BOOK

INTRODUCE THE TITLE AND AUTHOR Introduce students to the title and the author of *Tulips for Annie's Mother*. As students look at the cover illustration, ask: What do you think is going on in the drawing? What does this makes you imagine the selection is about?

BUILD BACKGROUND Discuss with students what they know about the Great Depression. Ask them if they ever moved or knew someone who had moved and how that made them feel.

PREVIEW/USE TEXT FEATURES Invite students to look at the illustrations in the story. Ask: What does the drawing on page 7 tell you about the adult pictured? Have students compare that picture with the illustration on page 12. Ask: Does this last illustration suggest what kind of ending this story might have?

READ THE BOOK

SET PURPOSE Have students set a purpose for reading *Tulips for Annie's Mother*. Students' interest in finding out how people lived and survived during the Great Depression should guide this purpose.

STRATEGY SUPPORT: STORY STRUCTURE Remind students that they are studying the sequence of the story. Suggest that as they read, students fill out the graphic organizers they created.

COMPREHENSION QUESTIONS

PAGE 4 What reminded Annie of the past? *(walking into her cold house)*

PAGE 5 What did Annie's father say was the cause of the Great Depression? *(Stocks lost their value and banks were out of money, so companies went out of business and people lost their jobs.)*

PAGE 8 Why do you think Annie's father never smiled? *(He was sad because he was out of work and couldn't provide for his family.)*

PAGE 9 In what way was Annie's family lucky? *(They had a farm so they had corn, potatoes, and fresh milk to sell and to eat.)*

REVISIT THE BOOK

READER RESPONSE

1. Possible responses: Cause: There was no money for heat. Effect: They had to wear sweaters. Cause: Annie's father got a job. Effect: He gave the children presents.
2. Possible responses: It takes place over a few days. Clue words: *the next morning.*
3. Sentences will vary.
4. Possible responses: People traded goods. People had each other over for supper.

EXTEND UNDERSTANDING Remind students that *plot,* what happens in a story, has a beginning, middle, and end. Ask students to map out the plot of *Tulips for Annie's Mother.*

RESPONSE OPTIONS

WRITING Have students imagine that they are Annie's mother. Ask them to write a journal entry about the day Annie's father gets a new job.

SOCIAL STUDIES CONNECTION

Discuss with students how music often helps people in difficult times. Explain that many songs came out of the Great Depression, and play the famous song "Brother, Can You Spare a Dime?" and hand out the lyrics. Ask: How do you think this song made people feel less alone during the Depression?

Skill Work

TEACH/REVIEW VOCABULARY

Provide students two sentences for each vocabulary word—one sentence that uses the word correctly and one sentence that uses the word incorrectly. Then tell students to read each sentence and mark it as either correct or incorrect.

ELL After reviewing vocabulary words with students, give them multiple definitions for each word and have them select the correct one.

TARGET SKILL AND STRATEGY

CAUSE AND EFFECT Remind students that *cause* is why something happened and *effect* is what happened. As they read, encourage students to ask: *What happened? Why did it happen?* Have students create a cause-and-effect graphic organizer for *Flowers for Annie's Mother.* Direct students to find at least three causes and three effects in the story.

STORY STRUCTURE Remind students that *story structure* is the way a story is organized. Explain that this story is organized chronologically, or in the order in which the events happen. Ask students to make a flowchart for *Tulips for Annie's Mother.* Tell students that as they read, they should put events in the order they happen and include all important events. Remind students that identifying the structure of a story can help them recognize causes and effects.

ADDITIONAL SKILL INSTRUCTION

AUTHOR'S PURPOSE Remind students that *author's purpose* is the reason an author writes a story, such as to entertain, to persuade, to express feelings, or to inform. Ask: Why do you think the author wrote *Tulips for Annie's Mother?* Suggest that as they read, students find details that support their answer.

Name _____

Cause and Effect

- An **effect** is something that happens. A **cause** is why that thing happened.
- Sometimes there are clue words or phrases to help you figure out what happened and why. Some of these clue words and phrases are *so, because, since, consequently,* and *as a result.*

Directions Read each of these sentences. Circle the cause and underline the effect.

1. Sue was moving, which made Annie feel sad.

2. Everyone joked at dinner because Annie's father now had a job.

3. Annie's family was lucky to have a farm because that meant they had food to eat.

4. Because it took hours to get food at the store, Annie's father was often late.

5. Companies went out of business, so people lost their jobs.

6. Annie's mother was sad because she had no money to buy flowers.

7. When the stock market crashed, stocks suddenly were worth nothing.

8. Annie's family was happy because Annie's father got a new job.

Directions Answer these questions.

9. What was the cause of the Great Depression?

_____

_____

_____

10. What were two effects of the Great Depression?

_____

_____

_____

Vocabulary

Directions Draw a line from each word to its definition.

```
┌─────────────────────────────────────┐
│   Check the Words You Know           │
│   ___beauty          ___blooming     │
│   ___bulbs           ___doze         │
│   ___humor           ___recognizing  │
│   ___showers         ___sprouting    │
└─────────────────────────────────────┘
```

1. beauty

2. blooming

3. bulbs

4. doze

5. humor

6. recognizing

7. sprouting

8. showers

a. nap

b. funny or amusing aspect

c. light rain

d. producing buds

e. knowing

f. kinds of seeds

g. very pretty

h. flowering

Directions Write a story about a garden using at least four vocabulary words.

_____

_____

_____

_____

_____

_____

_____

_____

_____

Pictures in the Sky

SUMMARY This informational text explains how ancient people named the constellations and made them a part of their culture. The text supports and extends the lesson concept of myths and nature.

LESSON VOCABULARY

antlers	imagined
language	narrator
overhead	poke

INTRODUCE THE BOOK

INTRODUCE THE TITLE AND AUTHOR Discuss with students the title and the author of *Pictures in the Sky*. Based on the title and cover illustration, ask students what kind of information they think this book will provide. Talk about how the ancient figure on the cover might relate to *Pictures in the Sky*.

BUILD BACKGROUND Explain that a constellation is a group of stars that forms a pattern. Discuss with students what they know about stars or constellation names.

PREVIEW/USE PHOTOGRAPHS AND CAPTIONS Have students preview the book by skimming the text and looking at the photos, drawings, diagrams, labels, and captions. Based on this preview, ask students what they expect to learn from reading this book. Talk about the sections of the book that they want to know more about.

ELL Ask volunteers to describe any special names in their home language for stars and constellations. Review any specific vocabulary words that may cause added difficulty for less-proficient English speakers.

READ THE BOOK

SET PURPOSE Have students set a purpose for reading. Draw their attention to the introduction on page 3 and discuss the fascination people have always had for stargazing. The constellation diagrams of animals may stimulate their interest.

STRATEGY SUPPORT: SUMMARIZE Explain that when we *summarize* something we've read, we include the most important details. Summarizing as we read helps us remember important details, which helps us understand what we've read. Suggest that small groups each take a section of the selection and write a brief statement summarizing it. Discuss these summaries as a class and together come up with one summarizing statement for the whole book.

COMPREHENSION QUESTIONS

PAGE 4 How were the patterns of constellations first determined? (*Ancient astronomers imagined the patterns.*)

PAGES 9–12 In what ways did the constellations help ancient people? (*The constellations explained wonders of nature and served as calendars for farmers.*)

PAGES 13–14 Why do people like the Native Americans or Africans make up legends about the constellations? (*Possible response: Stars are important to their lives.*)

REVISIT THE BOOK

READER RESPONSE

1. Possible response: to inform readers of how people made up stories about the stars

2. Main idea: Astronomers met to organize stars. Supporting details: placed night stars in constellations; created 88 constellations

3. overhead; Sentences will vary.

4. Some students may see the patterns. Ask them to explain how they see them.

EXTEND UNDERSTANDING Have students identify the constellation diagram in the book they like best and research it on the Internet or in reference books. Encourage them to look for other drawings of the constellation. Then ask them to make their own diagram based on their research.

RESPONSE OPTIONS

WRITING Provide additional books with information and photos of various constellations. Have students choose a constellation and write their own modern myth about it.

WORD WORK On page 10, students read that the word astronomy comes from Greek words. As a class, research Latin names associated with astronomy, and note that they are full of images like "ear of corn" or "female warrior." Discuss why stars may have so many names.

SCIENCE CONNECTION

Have students develop a "Myth vs. Reality" file for several constellations. Small groups of students can choose a constellation and develop a chart that explains the ancient myth surrounding it and factual information about its stars. Encourage them to illustrate the chart with an image of the constellation.

Skill Work

TEACH/REVIEW VOCABULARY

Discuss the vocabulary words with students. To reinforce word meaning, ask questions such as, "What are some animals that have antlers?" Have pairs of students take turns making up a similar question for each vocabulary word.

TARGET SKILL AND STRATEGY

AUTHOR'S PURPOSE Remind students that an author may write for different purposes—to inform, to persuade, to entertain, or to express feelings. Based on their previews, ask students what they think the *author's purpose* was for writing *Pictures in the Sky.*

SUMMARIZE Remind students that *summarizing* is a brief statement that focuses on the main ideas of a text and can help readers determine an author's purpose. For example, if the summary shows that the author is providing lots of facts, then the author's purpose is probably to inform. Stress that when students are uncertain about a section they have read, they should ask themselves questions such as, "What is this about? What does the author mean?" Understanding how the text is organized will help students summarize.

ADDITIONAL SKILL INSTRUCTION

MAIN IDEA While students may understand the concept of *main idea,* they often need practice finding that one big idea within a specific text. To find the main idea of *Pictures in the Sky,* students can consult the diagrams and captions. Help students understand that this book is organized around facts and descriptions about stars and constellations. To find the main idea among these facts, students may need to use a graphic organizer.

Author's Purpose

- The **author's purpose** is the reason or reasons an author has for writing.
- An author may have one or more reasons for writing. He or she may want *to inform, to persuade, to entertain,* or *to express* a mood or feeling.

Directions Read the passages and write the purpose you think the author had for writing each.

1. When was the last time you looked up at the night sky? Have you ever wanted to poke your finger through the stars in the night sky?

_____

2. It was a dark and stormy night when the old carriage wobbled along the cobbled path. "Just one star could give some light," the old driver whispered to himself. "If I could just see the dog star, I might be able to get through this long dark night."

_____

3. Each constellation has its own area of the sky. Many constellations were named after gods and heroes from Greek and Roman myths. People also like to name constellations after animals.

_____

4. We believe that pollution is disturbing the night sky. We need astronomers to help us. We want astronomers to show people why stars and their constellations are important to all humans. We need people to stop polluting the air. Please help us save the night sky.

_____

Directions Write a short paragraph about the stars. Choose one purpose for your paragraph. Write so that your purpose will be easily understood.

_____

_____

_____

_____

© Pearson Education 3

Name _____

Vocabulary

Directions Choose the word from the box that best matches each definition. Write the word on the line.

Check the Words You Know

___antlers   ___imagined   ___language
___narrator   ___overheard   ___poke

1. someone who tells a story _____

2. bony horns found on the head of an animal _____

3. words used to communicate _____

4. having formed an idea in the mind _____

5. to push with a finger against something _____

Directions Write the word from the box that belongs in each group.

6. pictured, made up _____

7. speech, communication _____

8. above, in the clouds _____

9. teller of tales, storyteller _____

10. push, jab _____

Directions Write a sentence using two words from the box.

_____

_____

_____

The First Year

SUMMARY This story explores how early settlers used their knowledge of nature, along with help from Native Americans, to prosper and survive in colonial Virginia. The story also shows students how people can learn to adapt to new surroundings and environments.

LESSON VOCABULARY

blade	budding
dew	fireflies
flutter	hawkmoth
notepad	patch

INTRODUCE THE BOOK

INTRODUCE THE TITLE AND AUTHOR Discuss with students the title and the author of *The First Year*. Based on the title, ask students what kind of information they think this book will provide. Ask: Why do you think the book was called *The First Year*? What images does this brings to mind? Direct students to look at the cover illustration to see more clues about the story's content. Guide them to pay attention to details in the illustration. Ask: Do these people look like they know each other? What time of year does it look like?

BUILD BACKGROUND Ask students if they have ever gone camping or if there was ever a time when the electricity or water didn't work in their homes. Discuss how they and their family had to improvise solutions, such as lighting candles or using bottled water. Also ask students if they have ever grown any fruits, vegetables, or plants, and discuss the work involved.

PREVIEW/USE TEXT FEATURES Invite students to take a picture walk through the illustrations. Ask them how the illustrations give clues to what is going to happen in the story.

READ THE BOOK

SET PURPOSE Have students set a purpose for reading *The First Year*. Students' curiosity about early settlers and how to survive in a new environment should guide this purpose. Suggest that as they read, students think about how much more difficult it was to live during that time.

STRATEGY SUPPORT: ASK QUESTIONS As they read, have students answer the questions they posed earlier. When they finish reading, ask students if they have more questions. Suggest they write their new questions and research the answers.

COMPREHENSION QUESTIONS

PAGE 5 What three things did Sarah and Jacob's father make with the trees and logs? *(a boat, a fire, notebooks for his children)*

PAGE 7 What conclusion can you draw about why Sarah wanted to plant more? *(She was excited to see the flowers blooming.)*

PAGE 7 If the garden bloomed with every color, what conclusion can you draw about what was planted? *(Lots of different seeds for colorful flowers were planted.)*

PAGE 9 What conclusion can you draw about how the Native Americans felt about the family? *(The Native Americans liked the family because the family helped them.)*

REVISIT THE BOOK

READER RESPONSE

1. Responses will vary.
2. Possible response: What kinds of games did you play? What was your journey to America like?
3. *note* and *pad*; Responses will vary.
4. Possible response: I would feel excited because I'd get to see new things.

EXTEND UNDERSTANDING Remind students that a *character* is the person who does the action in a story. Explain how details in a story tell many things about a character. Suggest students make a Venn diagram for Sarah and Jacob, using details from the story that show what the characters are like. Remind students that they can draw conclusions about Sarah and Jacob from their actions in the story.

RESPONSE OPTIONS

WRITING Have students imagine they are Sarah or Jacob during any of the seasons mentioned in the book. Ask students to write a journal entry about one day in this New Land. Have volunteers read their entries aloud to the class.

SOCIAL STUDIES CONNECTION

Ask students to research what life might have been like for this family in England and why they might have left to make a new home in America. Then invite students to make a graph and compare and contrast the family's life in England with that in America. If students are interested, ask them to compare their own lives with those of Sarah and Jacob.

Skill Work

TEACH/REVIEW VOCABULARY

Review the vocabulary words. Then play "Vocabulary Master" with students. Give students three different definitions for each vocabulary word, including one that is fantastical or silly, and have them select the correct definition. Then students can use the word in a sentence.

ELL Ask students to skim the story and write down any unfamiliar words. Suggest they look the words up in the dictionary and write the meanings in their notebooks.

TARGET SKILL AND STRATEGY

DRAW CONCLUSIONS Remind students that *drawing conclusions* means making a decision that makes sense after thinking about certain facts or details. Give students a few sentences about a topic related to this story, such as camping or making friends with strangers, and have them draw reasonable conclusions about that topic.

ASK QUESTIONS Remind students that *asking questions* is a way to further understand a topic and gain more information. Ask students what questions they have about the story they are about to read. Have students write their questions down; as they read, they can see if their questions are answered.

ADDITIONAL SKILL INSTRUCTION

PLOT Remind students that *plot* is the sequence of events that take a story from the beginning to the middle to the end. A plot often is about how someone solved a problem. Ask students to graph the plot of a story they have recently read, dividing the events into the categories of *beginning, middle,* and *end.* Suggest that students figure out the parts of the plot of *The First Year* as they read the story.

Draw Conclusions

- **Drawing conclusions** is thinking about facts or details and deciding something about them.
- It can also mean figuring something out by thinking about it.

Directions Read the following passage. Then answer the questions below.

> Tim had a new dog and he couldn't wait for his friend Doug to meet him. Tim called his dog Rascal. Rascal was pretty big and he liked to jump on people. When Doug saw Rascal, he didn't walk over and pet the dog. He didn't wave his hand to say "hello." Instead, he stayed by the door with his hands deep in his pockets. "Don't you want to pet my new dog?" Tim asked, astonished. Doug shook his head.
>
> "Maybe later," Doug said, and then looked at his watch. "I forgot something. I better go home." Doug left quickly.

1-2. Write two facts that show how Doug acted.

_____

_____

_____

3-4. Identify two facts about what Doug said.

_____

_____

_____

5. What can you conclude about how Doug feels about dogs?

_____

_____

_____

Name _____

Vocabulary

Directions Unscramble the words below. Then write their definitions.

Check the Words You Know

___blade	___budding	___dew	___fireflies
___flutter	___hawkmoth	___notepad	___patch

1. wed _____

_____

2. flieserif _____

_____

3. htacp _____

_____

4. ingbudd _____

_____

5. tertulf _____

_____

6. dapenot _____

_____

7. delba _____

_____

8. mothkwah _____

_____

Directions Write a sentence using one or more vocabulary words.

_____

_____

A Day With the Dogs

SUMMARY Dana likes to help her mom, a veterinarian at an animal shelter. On this snowy day, Dana spends her time with the dogs. Her favorite part is showing the dogs to people who want to adopt them. Dana also finds a lost dog in the snow—just in time.

LESSON VOCABULARY

anxiously	bay	blizzard
channel	chip	melody
supplies	surrounded	symphony

INTRODUCE THE BOOK

INTRODUCE THE TITLE AND AUTHOR Discuss with students the title and the author of *A Day With the Dogs*. Based on the title, discuss with students how this book might be related to the concept of helping animals in danger. Ask if students can tell by the title and cover illustration if it is a fiction or nonfiction book.

BUILD BACKGROUND Discuss what students know about animal shelters, and ask if any of them have adopted animals from one. Encourage students to describe their experiences at shelters and how people helped the animals there.

PREVIEW/USE ILLUSTRATIONS Suggest that students look at the illustrations to predict how the story will tell about a day with dogs. By looking at the pictures, can they describe how the girl helps the dogs?

READ THE BOOK

SET PURPOSE If necessary, go back to the material presented in *Build Background* to generate ideas from students as to why they may want to read this book. Most children like animals and may be interested in reading about other children helping them. Suggest that students may want to make up their own animal story after reading this one.

STRATEGY SUPPORT: ANSWER QUESTIONS The value in *answering questions* is to increase students' ability to provide complete and focused responses to questions. This strategy helps them make a generalization. You can ask students questions before, during, or after reading. Student responses should help them to continually monitor their comprehension as they read, as well as help them assess the book and its meaning at the end. Model how to answer some of the questions you raise.

COMPREHENSION QUESTIONS

PAGE 7 Why does Maria say that the dogs were wailing? *(They don't like the weather.)*

PAGE 9 What was difficult for Dana when she helped at the shelter? *(when dogs she loved were adopted)*

PAGE 13 Why did Dr. Tran wrap the lost dog in a blanket? *(The dog needed warmth.)*

PAGE 14 Even though the dog did not have a collar, why didn't Dana think he was a stray? *(Dana was careful to observe how the puppy looked and acted, and that made her wonder if the owner missed the dog.)*

REVISIT THE BOOK

READER RESPONSE

1. Responses will vary.
2. Possible response: They wrapped the puppy in warm towels and rubbed him softly.
3. Possible response: Dana was worried about the dog getting back to its owners.
4. Possible response: The chip identified the dog's owners; without it, the dog would have had to stay at the shelter.

EXTEND UNDERSTANDING Students may want to think about themselves as if they were in the character's place. Help students see that authors often write characters so that the reader can identify with them or want to be like them. Ask students what made the character of Dana believable. Their responses may help them in their writing the *Response Option*.

RESPONSE OPTIONS

WRITING Suggest that students use the questions they had from reading and research some aspect of caring for dogs or other animals in rescue situations. Divide the class into two groups—one group to write a story about children helping animals and another group to illustrate it.

SOCIAL STUDIES CONNECTION

Time For SOCIAL STUDIES

Students may want to research shelters or seeing eye dogs. If possible, have stories available of dogs helping humans.

TEACH/REVIEW VOCABULARY

Talk with students about how some words in a story create mood. Ask: How does the use of *blizzard* bring urgency to the story? Why might the sounds of a *symphony* help dogs in a shelter? Suggest that volunteers find the vocabulary words used in the story and make up their own sentences using these words.

ELL Ask students to work in pairs, each writing a different word and its definition on either side of an index card. Less-proficient English speakers can gain more facility with the vocabulary words by saying the word and its definition with help from more-proficient speakers.

TARGET SKILL AND STRATEGY

GENERALIZE As students read the book, have them look for the specific ways Dana, her mother, and Dr. Tran help the dogs. Suggest that students track this information by putting it in a cluster diagram around a central idea of *humans helping animals*. Then ask students to *generalize* about how people help animals.

ANSWER QUESTIONS Before students read, ask them questions to help them read with more focus. Then monitor their comprehension as they read. Remind students to draw on their own experience as they read this story, so that what they know about pets or animals from shelters can help them *answer questions* the author raises.

ADDITIONAL SKILL INSTRUCTION

CHARACTER Help students begin to make inferences about Dana's *character* by listing their ideas of what kind of person she is.

Name _____

Generalize

- When authors present one statement about many ideas or people, they are making a **generalization**.
- A generalization is a kind of conclusion.

Directions Use the graphic organizer to make a generalization based on *A Day With the Dogs*. Choose three details from the list below that go together. Write them in the Supporting Details boxes. Then write a generalization in the top box.

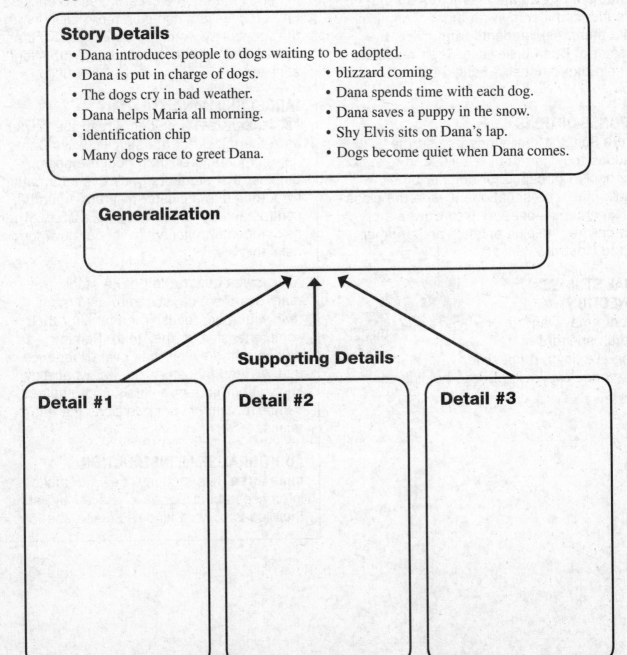

Story Details
- Dana introduces people to dogs waiting to be adopted.
- Dana is put in charge of dogs.
- The dogs cry in bad weather.
- Dana helps Maria all morning.
- identification chip
- Many dogs race to greet Dana.
- blizzard coming
- Dana spends time with each dog.
- Dana saves a puppy in the snow.
- Shy Elvis sits on Dana's lap.
- Dogs become quiet when Dana comes.

Generalization

Supporting Details

Detail #1

Detail #2

Detail #3

© Pearson Education 3

Vocabulary

Directions Read the sentences. Write the word from the box that means the same as the underlined word or phrase.

Check the Words You Know

___ anxiously	___ bay	___ blizzard
___ channel	___ chip	___ melody
___ supplies	___ surrounded	___ symphony

---

1. _____ Dana wanted to play a <u>simple tune</u> on a flute.

2. _____ Dana did not see any boats in the <u>narrow water passage</u>.

3. _____ All the dogs <u>encircled</u> Dana, begging for her attention.

4. _____ Dana's mother had to <u>scrape</u> the ice off her car windows.

5. _____ "This is scary," said Dana as she looked at the <u>snowstorm</u> outside.

6. _____ Dana felt sad to see that the dogs waited <u>nervously</u> in their cages for food and water.

7. _____ The whistling wind seemed to create a <u>whole concert</u> of sounds from nature.

8. _____ Marie made sure the veterinarians had the <u>necessary goods</u> to care for the sick animals.

9. _____ Dana's house was set off the <u>inlet</u> and down the road from the river.

Directions Write one sentence about *A Day With the Dogs* using as many vocabulary words as possible.

10. _____

_____

Mount St. Helens

SUMMARY This book gives readers information about the events prior to the eruption of Mount St. Helens and the aftermath of the explosion. Students will learn how science can help us prepare or protect ourselves from natural disasters.

LESSON VOCABULARY

beneath	buried
chimney	earthquakes
fireworks	force
tremble	volcanoes

INTRODUCE THE BOOK

INTRODUCE THE TITLE AND AUTHOR Discuss with students the title and the author of *Mount St. Helens*. Point out the "Earth Science" label on the cover. Ask students if they know what earth science is and how this book might fit into that category. Discuss what the picture on the cover makes students think about and why.

BUILD BACKGROUND Ask students: What do you know about natural disasters such as earthquakes and volcanoes? Discuss the reasons for these events and why they are called "disasters."

PREVIEW/USE TEXT FEATURES Preview with students the diagrams on page 6 and page 8 showing how a volcano erupts, and compare them with the photographs of a volcano on page 9. Ask students how the diagrams help them better understand what goes on when a volcanic eruption occurs.

READ THE BOOK

SET PURPOSE Have students set a purpose for reading *Mount St. Helens*. Students' curiosity and interest in volcanoes should guide this purpose.

STRATEGY SUPPORT: MONITOR AND FIX UP Discuss where students had problems understanding as they read. Ask: Did the read-on strategy help you? Why or why not?

COMPREHENSION QUESTIONS

PAGE 8 Could scientists tell when Mount St. Helens was going to erupt? *(No, but they knew it was coming.)*

PAGE 10 Why did Harry Truman refuse to leave the mountain? *(He didn't want to leave his home.)*

PAGES 14–15 Using the diagram, compare and contrast the various volcanoes. *(Possible responses: Tambora is the largest, El Chichon and Mount St. Helens look to be about the same size; Vesuvius was the earliest in A.D. 79, and Mount St. Helen's was the latest.)*

PAGE 15 Why was a monument put on Mount St. Helens? *(to remind people of the natural disaster)*

REVISIT THE BOOK

READER RESPONSE

1. Organizers will vary but should show that life has returned to many places where there had been landslides. Life has hardly come back at all where there had been lava flows. Overall, life is coming back to most parts of the mountain.
2. The bulge is first described on page 6.
3. Sample response: He watched the leaf *tremble*.
4. Students might answer that the map helped them see how close the Cascades are to the ocean, how they run in almost a straight line, etc.

EXTEND UNDERSTANDING Remind students that diagrams can help them understand complicated explanations. Direct students' attention to the diagram on page 11 that shows an erupting volcano. Based on what students have read, ask them to describe what is happening in the diagram and why.

RESPONSE OPTIONS

WRITING Ask students to imagine they are reporters. Have them write an eyewitness account of the eruption of Mount St. Helens, including the important facts of the event.

SCIENCE CONNECTION

Invite students to construct a model volcano out of clay.

Skill Work

TEACH/REVIEW VOCABULARY

Play a vocabulary game with students. Say: The word I'm thinking of has to do with something in a house where smoke escapes. What is it? (*chimney*) Give similar clues for each vocabulary word.

ELL Review vocabulary words with students and then give them a simple crossword puzzle of the vocabulary words that uses their definitions as clues.

TARGET SKILL AND STRATEGY

COMPARE AND CONTRAST Remind students that to *compare and contrast* is to look for likenesses and differences between objects, ideas, or pieces of text. Call attention to the diagram on pages 14 and 15. Model comparing and contrasting by asking such questions as "Which two eruptions were most similar? What is different about Vesuvius's eruption?"

MONITOR AND FIX-UP Tell students that *monitoring* their comprehension as they read means recognizing when the text stops making sense to them. *Fix-up* stategies improve comprehension and include rereading, reading on, and asking for help from someone. Encourage students to use whatever fix-up strategies they need when something in the text confuses them.

ADDITIONAL SKILL INSTRUCTION

GENERALIZE Remind students that generalizations are broad statements that apply to many examples. Point out that generalizations are often signaled by clue words such as *generally, seldom, few,* or *most*. Ask students to use these clue words to write generalizations that pertain to volcanoes or the weather.

Compare and Contrast

- To **compare** two or more things means to find their similarities and differences.
- To **contrast** two or more things means to find only their differences.

Directions In *Mount St. Helens*, you learned about how a volcano erupts. Compare and contrast the volcano before and after the eruption, using the chart below.

Before Eruption	After Eruption
1. _____ _____ _____	3. _____ _____ _____
2. _____ _____ _____	4. _____ _____ _____

5. What remained the same before and after the eruption of Mount St. Helens?

_____

_____

Name _____

Vocabulary

Directions Choose a word from the box that best completes each sentence.

Check the Words You Know			
___beneath	___buried	___chimney	___earthquakes
___fireworks	___force	___tremble	___volcanoes

1. Mount St. Helens _____ the town in ash.

2. When the volcano explodes, the ground will _____.

3. There are many _____ in Hawaii, but most are not active.

4. A volcano explodes with great _____.

5. California has had many destructive _____.

Directions Write a sentence using the vocabulary words below.

6. buried _____

_____

7. fireworks _____

_____

8. chimney _____

_____

9. surface _____

_____

10. beneath _____

_____

Brave Settlers in a Strange Land

SUMMARY *Brave Settlers in a Strange Land* describes a modern-day visit to Ellis Island by a grandfather and his grandchildren, who learn what it was like to immigrate to America through Ellis Island. They also learn a few facts about immigration today.

LESSON VOCABULARY

attention	complained
drifting	giggle
glaring	looping
struggled	swooping

INTRODUCE THE BOOK

INTRODUCE THE TITLE AND AUTHOR Discuss with students the title and the author of *Brave Settlers in a Strange Land*. Point out the cover illustration to students. Talk about who the people in the picture might be and what sort of trip they are making.

BUILD BACKGROUND Talk with students about what the word *immigrant* means to them. Have students suggest what they know about immigrants, either from their own family experiences or from books and movies. Define the word for students, and discuss where immigrants to the United States have come from.

ELL Ask volunteers among ELL students to describe the experiences of their families immigrating to America. Have the students describe what it was like to leave their homelands and adapt to a strange environment with a new language and culture.

PREVIEW/USE TEXT FEATURES Have students skim through the book, looking at the pictures and captions. Explain that the subject of the book is Ellis Island, a place that used to be the main entry point for immigrants to the United States. Point out that Ellis Island is now a museum.

READ THE BOOK

SET PURPOSE Review with students what the word "immigrant" means to them. Tell students to consider those ideas and the subject of the book, Ellis Island. Have each student set a purpose for reading that answers the question: What I want to know about immigrants and Ellis Island is _____.

STRATEGY SUPPORT: ANSWER QUESTIONS To help students understand how to answer questions, have them write the following headings on a piece of paper: Where I Looked in the Text and What I Knew. As students find the answer to question 1 from Reader Response, have them write down how they found the answer to the question.

COMPREHENSION QUESTIONS

PAGE 5 Grandpa said America has been called a "melting pot." What caused people to use this term? *(Americans expected people who came from other parts of the world to "melt" into society.)*

PAGE 9 Why does Grandpa think that his grandmother must have felt lonely? Use the text and your own knowledge to answer the question. *(Possible response: She couldn't speak English or the languages of her neighbors. She probably didn't have many friends.)*

PAGE 11 What do you think is the author's purpose in telling about Native Americans? *(Possible response: to inform the reader that the Native Americans were the first people in this country; to persuade the reader that everyone who came after the Native Americans is an immigrant)*

PAGE 13 What causes most new immigrants to come to America through California? *(California is closer to the countries where the new immigrants are coming from.)*

REVISIT THE BOOK

READER RESPONSE

1. Possible response: They had to pass a medical exam and show documents.
2. Possible response: Immigrants were expected to give up their cultures to fit in; page 5.
3. Answers will vary.
4. I would feel lonely and scared.

EXTEND UNDERSTANDING Point out that authors often use graphic sources, such as time lines, maps, graphs, and photographs to further explain information in a text. Have students look at the chart on page 9 and discuss how this graphic source helps them understand the information in the text. Also, have students suggest other graphic sources that the author might have included in the text and explain why those graphics would have aided the reader.

RESPONSE OPTIONS

WRITING Have students create new graphic sources for the selection. Possibilities include a time line of immigration, a graph of immigrants by place of origin, or a map of immigration patterns. Provide students with models of each type of graphic. Have students use information from the text to fill in their graphics.

SOCIAL STUDIES CONNECTION

Provide students with first-hand accounts, either from books or the Internet, of immigrants who entered America through Ellis Island. Have each student write a brief biography of his or her immigrant explaining where the person was from, what their trip to America was like, and what happened when they arrived in the United States. Have students share their biographies with the class.

Skill Work

TEACH/REVIEW VOCABULARY

Have pairs of students use the glossary to write the vocabulary words and their definitions on separate index cards. Tell pairs to turn all the index cards facedown and play "concentration," where each partner takes a turn turning over the cards and matching the words with their definitions. Have partners keep time for each other and play the game trying to beat their own best times.

TARGET SKILL AND STRATEGY

CAUSE AND EFFECT Remind students that an *effect* in a book is what happens, and a *cause* is why that event happens. Students might look for the clue words *because* and *so*. Remind students that an author might not use clue words to identify a cause-and-effect relationship. Have students look for two examples of cause and effect in the story.

ANSWER QUESTIONS Remind students that a question might have an answer right in the pages of the story. Other times a question will require readers to use their own prior knowledge to figure out what an author means, not just what the author writes. Have students read question 1 in Reader Response and identify how they might answer the question.

ADDITIONAL SKILL INSTRUCTION

AUTHOR'S PURPOSE Explain that *author's purpose* is the reason an author writes a book. Point out that authors usually have more than one of the following reasons for writing: to entertain, inform, persuade, or express a mood or feeling. Since the selection is about a real place, Ellis Island, ask students what they think is the main reason the author wrote the book (*to inform the reader about Ellis Island*). As they read, have students think about another purpose the author may have had for writing the story.

Name _____

Cause and Effect

- A **cause** is why something happened. An **effect** is what happened.

Directions Read each of the following effects in *Brave Settlers in a Strange Land.*
For each effect, write a cause.

1. Today's immigrants are not expected to "melt," or fit, into society as much as they used to be.

Cause _____

_____

2. Immigrants like Grandpa's grandmother used to face a lot of prejudice.

Cause _____

3. Grandpa's grandmother could not talk to most of her neighbors.

Cause _____

_____

4. The United States has become a very diverse country.

Cause _____

_____

5. Many immigrants used to be frightened when they had to pass a medical exam and show documents.

Cause _____

_____

Name _____

Vocabulary

Directions Choose the word from the box that best matches each definition. Write the word on the line.

Check the Words You Know

___attention
___complained
___drifting
___giggle
___glaring
___looping
___struggled
___swooping

1. tried hard; worked hard against difficulties _____

2. said that you were unhappy, annoyed, or upset about something

   _____

3. staring angrily _____

4. careful thinking, looking, or listening _____

5. forming a line, path, or motion shaped so that it crosses itself _____

Directions Write the word from the box that belongs in each group.

6. laugh, chuckle, _____

7. dipping, diving, _____

8. floating, sailing, _____

9. objected, protested, _____

10. awareness, notice, _____

Getting the Lay of the Land

SUMMARY This nonfiction reader describes some of the different devices used to measure various land forms. For example, the book explains how satellites are used to measure the heights of mountains and how sonar is used to measure the depths of the oceans.

LESSON VOCABULARY

average	depth
desert	outrun
peak	tides
waterfalls	

INTRODUCE THE BOOK

INTRODUCE THE TITLE AND AUTHOR Discuss with students the title and the author of *Getting the Lay of the Land.* Based on the picture on the cover, have students suggest what types of land they think the book will be about. Then invite students to make educated guesses about what the title means.

BUILD BACKGROUND Have students brainstorm answers to the following questions: How do you think people measure the height of mountains? How do you think people measure the depth of the ocean? *(Responses will vary.)* Explain that *Getting the Lay of the Land* is a book about how people measure land forms. Have students suggest other questions they have about measuring features of Earth's surface.

PREVIEW/USE TEXT FEATURES Tell students to look through the book, paying special attention to the section headings. Ask: What types of land forms and measurements does this book talk about? *(heights of mountains, depths of oceans, directions, earthquakes, minerals)*

READ THE BOOK

SET PURPOSE Remind students that usually the main purpose of a nonfiction text is to inform the reader about a topic. Have students think about the headings in the book and set a purpose for reading by completing the following statement: *I would like to read this book to learn more about _____.*

STRATEGY SUPPORT: ASK QUESTIONS In comparing two measuring devices in the book, have students ask themselves the following questions: How are these two things the same? How are these two things different? Point out that students also may ask questions of their own to help them compare devices.

COMPREHENSION QUESTIONS

PAGE 5 Is the height of Mount Everest a fact or an opinion? How do you know? *(fact; it can be proved true or false)*

PAGE 7 What question could you ask that is answered on this page? *(Possible response: How do scientists measure the depth of the ocean?)*

PAGES 11 How do scientists find the exact location of an earthquake? *(measure the earthquake's distance from three cities that use seismographs)*

PAGES 12–13 Use the Mohs scale to compare and contrast quartz and topaz. How are these minerals alike? How are they different? *(Possible responses: They are alike because they are both harder than feldspar; they are different because quartz is softer than topaz.)*

REVISIT THE BOOK

READER RESPONSE

1. Possible responses: *Old Method:* uses a knotted rope and a weight, measured the rope; *New Method:* uses sound waves, measures travel time of the sound waves; *Both Methods:* send something to the ocean floor from a boat

2. Possible response: At the beginning of page 9, I wondered what made the numbers on an odometer change. I read on to learn that it's the axle.

3. page 8: *outrun*; page 9: *waterfalls*

4. Possible response: It shows how hard minerals are in relation to other minerals.

EXTEND UNDERSTANDING Point out that authors often use graphic sources, like *charts, graphs,* and *maps,* to help the reader understand information in the text. Review with students the graphic sources on pages 10, 11, and 12. Discuss with students how these graphics helped them understand how seismographs and the Mohs Scale work.

RESPONSE OPTIONS

WRITING Invite students to think of another measuring device that people use, such as a *thermometer, scale, ruler,* or *measuring cup.* Have students write a paragraph in which they compare and contrast their measuring device with one of the devices in the selection. Remind students to think of all the features that the two devices have in common and the features that are different.

SCIENCE CONNECTION

Provide groups of students with topographical maps of places around the world. Have groups think of five questions to ask others about their map. Then have students exchange maps and try to answer another group's questions. Remind each group that it needs to provide answers to its questions.

Skill Work

TEACH/REVIEW VOCABULARY

Read through the Glossary with students. Pair students for a game called "10 Tries." Have one student draw on a piece of paper the number of blanks that correspond to letters in one of the vocabulary words and write the definition beneath the blanks. The partner tries to guess the word by guessing letters. The goal is to guess the word before 10 tries are exhausted. Partners should take turns choosing a word and guessing.

TARGET SKILL AND STRATEGY

COMPARE AND CONTRAST Remind students that when they *compare* two or more things, they are describing how those things are alike. When they *contrast* those things, they are talking only about how they are different. Have students choose two measuring devices from the book to compare and contrast. Then have students think about how these devices are alike and different.

ELL Help students complete a Venn diagram to compare two of the measuring devices in the book.

ASK QUESTIONS Point out to students that when they *ask questions* about a text, they help themselves better understand and remember what they read. Remind students that they can ask questions to compare and contrast things in a story. Have students ask themselves questions as they compare and contrast two measuring devices in the book.

ADDITIONAL SKILL INSTRUCTION

FACT AND OPINION Review with students that *facts* are statements that can be proved true or false, while *opinions* are statements that tell someone's feelings or ideas about something. Discuss with students ways that facts may be proved true or false (checking in books, observing, asking experts). Point out some clue words that often indicate opinions, such as *best, worst, most, always, should.* Invite students to look for examples of one fact and one opinion as they read.

Name _____

Compare and Contrast

- A **comparison** shows how two or more things are alike. A **contrast** shows how two or more things are different.

- Clue words such as **like** and **as** show comparisons. Clue words such as **but** and **unlike** show contrasts.

Directions Complete the Venn diagram below to compare and contrast a Global Positioning System with a seismograph. Use information from *Getting the Lay of the Land* to help you complete the diagram.

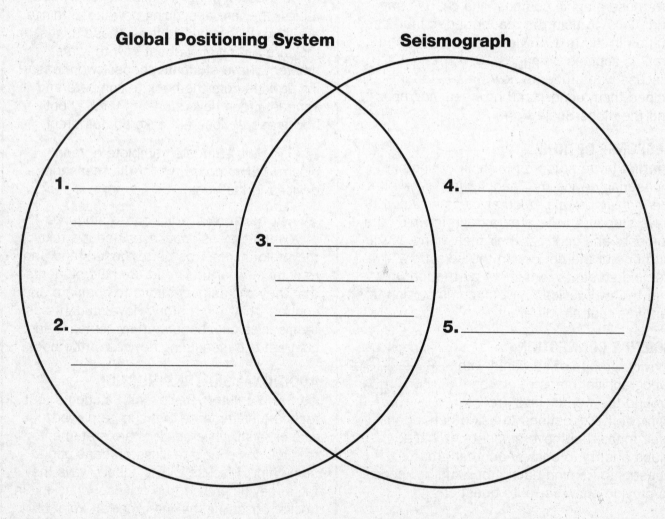

Global Positioning System   **Seismograph**

1. _____

_____

2. _____

_____

3. _____

_____

_____

4. _____

_____

5. _____

_____

_____

Name _____

Vocabulary

Directions Write the word from the word box that best matches each clue.

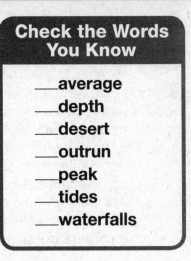

Check the Words You Know

___average
___depth
___desert
___outrun
___peak
___tides
___waterfalls

_____ 1. streams of water that fall from high places

_____ 2. a place where trees do not grow

_____ 3. the highest place on a mountain

_____ 4. the Moon and the Sun cause these

_____ 5. to move faster than something else

Directions Write the word or words from the box above that best fit each category.

6. Plural nouns _____

7. Verb _____

8. Words about water _____

9. Words about measuring _____

10. Things that move _____

Fun with Science!

SUMMARY In *Fun with Science!*, the author introduces readers to a few of the ways in which some popular hobbies are related to science. This nonfiction reader describes how bird watching, learning about the past, and stargazing resemble the scientific fields of zoology, archaeology, and astronomy. The author suggests how these hobbies could even lead to careers in science.

LESSON VOCABULARY

attic	board	chores
customers	label	spare
stamps		

INTRODUCE THE BOOK

INTRODUCE THE TITLE AND AUTHOR Discuss with students the title and the author of *Fun with Science!* Ask students what the boy in the cover photograph seems to be doing. (Possible response: looking at birds with binoculars) Discuss how this boy might be having "fun with science."

BUILD BACKGROUND Ask students to describe some of their own hobbies. Tell students that the selection they are about to read will describe some hobbies and how they are related to science.

ELL Have students talk about some hobbies or things people do in their spare time in their home countries. Suggest that students give examples of hobbies that are typical of their home countries but are uncommon in the United States.

PREVIEW/USE TEXT FEATURES Have students look through the book, focusing particularly on the headings. Discuss what sciences are mentioned in the headings. Invite students to talk about what the young people in the photographs appear to be doing and whether their activities look like any of the hobbies students mentioned in Build Background.

READ THE BOOK

SET PURPOSE Have students think of something they would like to know about a hobby and how it relates to science. Direct students to set one of the things they want to know about hobbies as their purpose for reading.

STRATEGY SUPPORT: PRIOR KNOWLEDGE Have each student create a KWL chart with the headings, What I Know, What I Would Like to Know, and What I Learned. As a class, fill in the first column of the chart with what students already know about hobbies related to science. Then have individual students fill in the second column of the chart with topics they would like to know about science-related hobbies. Tell students that when they finish reading, they will complete the third column with what they learned from the selection.

COMPREHENSION QUESTIONS

PAGE 5 Find a generalization that the author makes. (Possible responses: They come in many different shapes, sizes, and colors; some hummingbirds are only two inches long!)

PAGE 6 What do you know about birds that helps you understand the information? (Possible response: I already know that birds are afraid of people and fly away from them.)

PAGES 8–9 Find a generalization the author makes on these pages. (Possible responses: Old and ancient items are found every day in many different places; people sometimes like to save old items.)

PAGES 10–11 Use the text and captions on this page to help you draw a conclusion about where treasures from the past may be found. (Possible response: Treasures from the past may be found almost anywhere people live.)

PAGE 13 Make your own generalization about telescopes. (Possible response: Telescopes of any size are good tools for studying the stars.)

REVISIT THE BOOK

READER RESPONSE

1. Possible response: Telescopes and binoculars make objects appear larger.
2. Possible responses: Knew: They are scientists. Know now: Archaeologists dig for old things in the dirt. Want to learn: What kinds of things do archaeologists find?
3. Chores, customers, stamps; sentences will vary.
4. about two inches; up to eight feet

EXTEND UNDERSTANDING

Once students have finished reading the selection, have them fill in the L column in their KWL charts. Invite volunteers to share some of the items in their Want to Know and Learned columns. Then have students add a fourth column entitled Still Want to Know. Tell students to fill in things they would still like to find out about science-related hobbies. Invite volunteers to share items from their S columns, and discuss as a class where students might look for more information.

RESPONSE OPTIONS

WRITING Have students write a paragraph describing a favorite hobby. Tell them to include in their paragraphs the materials and activities involved in their hobbies and a sentence explaining why they enjoy doing these things in their spare time.

SCIENCE CONNECTIONS

Provide students with a list and brief descriptions of some scientific fields, such as physics, chemistry, biology, and ecology. Have students put their hobbies in concept webs or charts and write the different ways their hobbies relate to science. Provide some examples, such as how stamp collecting can tell a person something about the past and how baseball uses physics. Have students share their webs or charts with the class.

Skill Work

TEACH/REVIEW VOCABULARY

Read through the Glossary with students. Have students work in small groups to write a paragraph about what some people like to do in their spare time. Tell them to use each of the vocabulary words at least once in their paragraphs. Invite groups to share their paragraphs with the class.

TARGET SKILL AND STRATEGY

GENERALIZE Remind students that sometimes they can make a general statement about several ideas or things in a book. The statement can tell how the ideas or things are all alike or mostly alike, or how they are mostly different. Read the first paragraph of the selection on page 3 with students. Point out that in the last sentence, the author makes a general statement about hobbies: "There are many ways to spend spare time!" This sentence *generalizes* how all the activities in the paragraph are alike. As they read, have students think about a generalization they can make about the hobbies mentioned in the story.

PRIOR KNOWLEDGE Remind students that thinking about what they already know about a topic can help them understand what they read. Suggest that if students use *prior knowledge,* they will be able to make better generalizations about the facts in the text. As students read, have them note at least one instance where they activate prior knowledge to help them understand the text.

ADDITIONAL SKILL INSTRUCTION

DRAW CONCLUSIONS Point out that when readers make decisions about the facts in a book, they are *drawing conclusions.* As they read, have students think about the facts related to one of the hobbies in the selection. Tell students to use these facts to draw a conclusion about one of the hobbies discussed in the book.

Generalize

- A **generalization** is a broad statement or rule that applies to many examples.
- A **valid generalization** is adequately supported by specific facts and by logic.

Directions Fill in the chart below with facts about the science hobbies mentioned in *Fun with Science!* Then use the facts to make a generalization about hobbies connected to science. The first box has been done for you.

Generalization Chart: Facts About Hobbies Connected to Science

Bird Watching
1. You can use binoculars to watch birds.
2. _____
Digging into the Past
3. _____
4. _____
Star-Gazing
5. _____
6. _____
Generalization about science hobbies:
_____
_____

Name _____

Vocabulary

Directions Use each of the following words in a sentence about hobbies.

1. chores _____

2. label _____

3. attic _____

4. stamps _____

5. board _____

6. customers _____

Directions Put each group of words in alphabetical order.

7. customers, stamps, chores, spare _____

8. label, attic, customers, board _____

9. spare, chores, label, hobby _____

10. telescope, attic, spare, binoculars _____

Women Who Made a Difference

SUMMARY This nonfiction reader provides brief biographies of three women who broke down barriers against their gender in the early twentieth century: Babe Didrikson Zaharias, Amelia Earhart, and Eleanor Roosevelt.

LESSON VOCABULARY

celebrate	continued
current	drowned
medal	stirred
strokes	

INTRODUCE THE BOOK

INTRODUCE THE TITLE AND AUTHOR Discuss the title and the author of *Women Who Made a Difference.* Point out that this is a biography. Discuss with students what a biography is, and have them predict who this biography is about, based on the cover illustration.

BUILD BACKGROUND Discuss with students some of the activities that their mothers, grandmothers, and aunts perform in their daily lives, including work outside the house. Then, have girls in the class describe some of the things they like to do outside of school and what they plan to do in the future. Have boys in the class tell what their sisters, female cousins, or female friends do in their spare time. Ask students if girls can do the same things as boys do. Point out that not long ago, society believed there were certain things women should not do, such as vote.

ELL Have ELL students describe the social roles of women in their home countries and compare them to women's roles in the United States.

PREVIEW/USE TEXT FEATURES Have students skim through the book and describe some of the activities the women are doing in the pictures. Invite students to make predictions about what types of women are featured in this biography.

READ THE BOOK

SET PURPOSE Turn to page 3 of the reader, and read together with students the names of the women who are featured in the book. Guide students to set their own *purposes* for reading by having them decide which woman they would like to learn more about.

STRATEGY SUPPORT: MONITOR AND FIX UP Tell students that as they finish reading about each woman in the text, they should stop to write brief notes to support their comprehension. Have students use a *Main Idea and Supporting Details* graphic organizer to take notes about the women in the book. Point out that students should focus on the author's statements of fact as they look for details to note.

COMPREHENSION QUESTIONS

PAGES 4–5 Name one statement of fact and one statement of opinion you see on these pages. How do you know which is which? *(Possible responses: Fact: Babe Didrikson Zaharias was born in Texas in 1911. Opinion: She knew she was just as strong as any boy. The fact can be checked in a book. The opinion is just Babe's belief about herself.)*

PAGE 9 What is the main idea of this page? *(Possible response: Amelia Earhart proved that women could do daring things.)*

PAGE 11 Did you find anything confusing on this page? How did you fix up your understanding? *(Possible response: I didn't know what polio was. I read on and found that Eleanor became Franklin's nurse and saw in the picture that he couldn't walk. I guessed that polio is a disease.)*

PAGE 13 After reading this page, what do you think is the main idea of this book? *(Possible response: There are great women in history who worked hard to gain respect for all women.)*

REVISIT THE BOOK

READER RESPONSE

1. Possible responses: Fact: She was born on July 24, 1897, in Kansas. I can check an encyclopedia. Opinion: Most people didn't think that women should fly planes. This is a statement of the author's ideas or beliefs.

2. Possible response: Babe Didrikson Zaharias was a champion in several sports. Amelia Earhart was the first woman to fly a plane across the Atlantic Ocean by herself. Eleanor Roosevelt helped the poor and spoke out for the rights of women and minorities.

3. *Current:* a flow of water. The current pulled our boat upstream. *Strokes:* acts of striking. It took three strokes of the hammer to drive in the nail.

4. I think Amelia Earhart was the most daring because she flew across an ocean alone.

EXTEND UNDERSTANDING Point out to students that biographies are often about exceptional people, or people who have done exceptional things. Explain to students that authors may use adjectives in their biographies to express to the reader just how important the subject is. Have students look through the book for adjectives that Megan Litwin uses to describe the women in this biography. Discuss how the adjectives help the reader appreciate the accomplishments of these women.

RESPONSE OPTIONS

WRITING Have students write brief biographies of people that they consider important in their lives, such as a relative, teacher, or coach. Remind students to use main ideas and supporting details to describe their subjects, as well as statements of fact and opinion.

SOCIAL STUDIES CONNECTION

Have students research other important women in history. Tell students to write reports and include information about each person's childhood, special obstacles, and accomplishments. Remind students to include paragraphs about why these women are important to remember.

Skill Work

TEACH/REVIEW VOCABULARY

Write the vocabulary words on the chalkboard. Form groups, and assign one word to each. Have each group find its word in the book. Tell students to create word webs for their words based on context clues in the book. Have groups share their webs and check their definitions against the Glossary.

TARGET SKILL AND STRATEGY

FACT AND OPINION Explain to students that a *statement of fact* is a statement that can be proved true or false. A *statement of opinion* is a person's beliefs or ideas about something. Remind students that they just need to know that the statement *can* be checked by looking in reference sources, by asking an expert, or by observing. Give examples of statements of facts and opinions, and discuss with students how to distinguish each. Then tell students to list one statement of fact and one statement of opinion for each of the three women profiled in the reader.

MONITOR AND FIX UP Review with students that they should *monitor* their reading, or check their understanding of the text. Remind students that when they don't understand something, they can use a strategy to *"fix up"* their reading, such as writing notes to summarize. Explain that using monitor and fix-up strategies may help them understand facts and opinions in the text. Tell students to help fix up their comprehension by writing brief notes to summarize the facts about each woman in the reader.

ADDITIONAL SKILL INSTRUCTION

MAIN IDEA AND DETAILS Review with students that the *main idea* is the most important idea about a topic of a passage or a selection. Supporting *details* are the smaller pieces of information about the main idea. Tell students to look for the main idea about each woman in the reader and find two details that support this idea.

Name _____

Fact and Opinion

- A **statement of fact** is a statement that can be proved true or false. You can check a statement of fact by looking in reference sources, asking an expert, or observing.

- A **statement of opinion** is a person's beliefs or ideas about something. You cannot prove whether it is true or false.

Directions Read the following passage. Then answer the questions below.

In 1932, Babe went to the Olympic Games in Los Angeles. She set a world record in the javelin throw. Newspapers called her the "World's Greatest Athlete." Babe knew she could do anything she could put her mind to.

Next, Babe took up golfing. Her golf strokes were so strong that she became a champion at that too. In 1950, she was named the Outstanding Woman Athlete of the Half-Century. She died of cancer at a young age, but her memory and courage will live forever.

1. What is one statement of fact that the author makes in this passage?

_____

2. Where could you check whether the statement is true or false?

_____

3. What is one statement of opinion that the author makes in this passage?

_____

4. How do you know that this is a statement of opinion?

_____

_____

5. Which sentence in this passage contains both a statement of fact and a statement of opinion? Which part is which?

_____

_____

_____

Vocabulary

Directions Choose the word from the box that best matches each definition. Write the letters of the word on the lines.

> ## Check the Words You Know
>
> ___celebrate ___continued ___current ___drowned
> ___medal ___stirred ___strokes

1. awakened or brought to the surface __ __ __ __ __ __
                       1   2

2. to make known or famous __ __ __ __ __ __ __ __ __
            3

3. a small piece of metal, usually with a special design, given as an award for some outstanding act __ __ __ __ __
            4

4. went on in some action __ __ __ __ __ __ __ __ __
            5

5. in tennis, golf, etc., several strikings of the ball __ __ __ __ __ __ __
            6

6. died by suffocation in water __ __ __ __ __ __ __
            7

Directions Write down the letters from the numbered spaces above. Then unscramble the letters to form a word from the box. Use the word to answer the riddle below.

What word describes an event that is happening today?

7. _____

Directions Write sentences as directed below.

8. Use the word *stirred* in a sentence about cooking.

_____

_____

9. Use the word *celebrate* in a sentence about your favorite holiday.

_____

_____

The Lost Dog

SUMMARY This is a fictional story about a dog finding its way home over a great distance by using natural instincts and a keen sense of smell.

LESSON VOCABULARY

clutched	echoed
gully	reeds
scrambled	valley

INTRODUCE THE BOOK

INTRODUCE THE TITLE AND AUTHOR Discuss with students the title and author of *The Lost Dog*. Ask students what the title makes them imagine the story is about. Direct students' attention to the cover illustration and ask students how the illustration adds to the information the title gives them.

BUILD BACKGROUND Ask students if they have ever had a pet that got lost or if they have ever known anyone who had a pet that got lost. Discuss how the owner of the pet felt and what he or she did to get the dog back. Ask students if they have ever noticed the way dogs always sniff the ground, which can lead to a discussion of dogs' excellent sense of smell.

PREVIEW/USE TEXT FEATURES Suggest that students look at all the illustrations in the story. Ask students what the illustrations make them imagine the story is about. Direct students' attention to the drawings on page 7 and on page 15 and ask them how the expression on the character's face gives them clues as to what is happening in the story.

READ THE BOOK

SET PURPOSE Have students set a purpose for reading *The Lost Dog*. Students' curiosity and interest in dogs and their natural instincts should guide this purpose.

STRATEGY SUPPORT: GRAPHIC ORGANIZERS Suggest that as students read *The Lost Dog*, they create two or three graphic organizers to enhance their understanding of the story. For example, they could use a story map for the plot; a time line for the sequence of events; character webs to describe Sam, Buddy, and Mr. Hall; or a problem-and-solution or cause-and-effect chart to understand the action in the story.

COMPREHENSION QUESTIONS

PAGE 3 Even though this is the beginning of the story, there is also an ending on this page. What is it? *(It is the end of Sam's vacation with Alan and Alan's family.)*

PAGES 8–11 Using a graphic organizer, list what things Sam did to try and find Buddy. *(He called for him, he put up a notice, he left small pieces of his clothing for Buddy to find the scent.)*

PAGE 14 Why was Sam hopeful after he read about beagles? *(He learned that beagles were very good at following a scent.)*

PAGE 15 Were you surprised by the ending of the story? Why or why not? *(Possible response: I was surprised because I thought the dog was really lost. I was not surprised because I learned beagles could follow scents, and Sam had thrown out pieces of his clothes so Buddy could follow the scent.)*

REVISIT THE BOOK

READER RESPONSE

1. Possible responses: Sam, his friend Alan, and Sam's dog Buddy took a walk near their mountain cabin. Buddy chased a rabbit and got lost. Buddy found his way back home by following a scent trail that Sam left.
2. Possible responses: Cause: Rabbit is startled. Effect: Rabbit runs out of grass. Cause: Rabbit runs out of grass. Effect: Buddy chases the rabbit. Cause: Buddy chases the rabbit. Effect: Buddy gets lost.
3. Students should include *valley, reeds, gully,* and *echoed* in their descriptions.
4. Possible response: I have a dog. Some pets can run and play.

EXTEND UNDERSTANDING Remind students that the character is the person who talks and does the action in a story. Discuss the character of Sam with students. Using a Venn diagram, ask students to fill in details that show what kind of person Sam is.

RESPONSE OPTIONS

WRITING Ask students to imagine they are Sam and to create a commercial asking Buddy to come home. Students can also design a "LOST" poster if they are interested.

SCIENCE CONNECTION

Invite students to research another dog with a strong sense of smell, such as a bloodhound, and ask them to write and illustrate a report on that breed.

Skill Work

TEACH/REVIEW VOCABULARY

Review vocabulary words with students. Then write out the words with some of the letters missing, and invite students to name the vocabulary word. Do this with all the vocabulary words, and then have students use each word in a sentence.

ELL Review vocabulary words with students. Personalize each word by asking them questions such as, "If I were in a valley, where would I be?" Do the same for the remaining vocabulary words.

TARGET SKILL AND STRATEGY

PLOT AND THEME Remind students that the *plot* is the sequence of events in a story and that every story has a beginning, middle, and an end. Point out that every story also has a big idea, which is something that you learn from reading the story. Discuss a story the students are familiar with, and ask them to discuss the beginning, middle, and end, and the big idea of the story. Have students do the same as they read *The Lost Dog*.

GRAPHIC ORGANIZERS Remind students that *graphic organizers* can help them organize their thoughts about the information in a story. Encourage students to make a graphic organizer labeled "beginning events," "middle events," and "end events" that they can fill in as they read *The Lost Dog*. Remind students that the organizer can help them determine the parts of the plot and the big idea of the story.

ADDITIONAL SKILL INSTRUCTION

SEQUENCE OF EVENTS Remind students that sequence of events is the order in which things happen in a story. Sometimes clue words such as *first, then,* or *finally* help identify the sequence. Invite students to make a timeline of events in a story they know. Then ask them to use a timeline to map out sequence as they read *The Lost Dog*.

Plot and Theme

- The **plot** is the series of events in a story. These events can be divided into 3 parts—the beginning, the middle, and the end.
- The **theme** of a story is the big idea. It is what the author would like you to learn.

Directions Reread *The Lost Dog* and then fill in the graphic organizer.

Title _____

```
┌─────────────────────────────────────────────────────────┐
│  1. Beginning  What is the problem in the story?          │
│                                                           │
│                                                           │
│                                                           │
└─────────────────────────────────────────────────────────┘
                            │
                            ▼
┌─────────────────────────────────────────────────────────┐
│  2. Middle  What did Sam do to try to solve the problem?  │
│                                                           │
│                                                           │
│                                                           │
└─────────────────────────────────────────────────────────┘
                            │
                            ▼
┌─────────────────────────────────────────────────────────┐
│  3. End  How did Sam solve his problem?                   │
│                                                           │
│                                                           │
│                                                           │
└─────────────────────────────────────────────────────────┘
```

4. What do you think is the big idea of *The Lost Dog?*

_____

5. How do you know?

_____

_____

Vocabulary

Directions Find the vocabulary words from the box hidden in the word search below.

Check the Words You Know

___clutched
___echoed
___gully
___reeds
___scrambled
___valley

```
Q E H L J S N R V
A C L U T C H E D
M H B Y I R L E P
F O K U N A Q D O
G E Q T I M X S Z
R D L P F B G H C
B C V A L L E Y Q
N A X S R E Q S N
J V M F K D O L C
O K G U L L Y X V
```

Directions Use each word below in a sentence.

gully   scrambled   clutched   valley

1. _____

_____

2. _____

_____

3. _____

_____

4. _____

_____

Dressed for School Success

SUMMARY This selection gives students facts about what students in other cultures have worn to school over the centuries and around the world. It gives students a great opportunity to compare and contrast cultures.

LESSON VOCABULARY

cotton	festival
graceful	handkerchief
pale	pace
rhythm	snug

INTRODUCE THE BOOK

INTRODUCE THE TITLE AND AUTHOR Discuss with students the title and the author of *Dressed for School Success*. Direct students' attention to the term *social studies* in the triangle on the cover and ask them how they imagine the way you dress is part of social studies. Ask students why they think the reader is called *Dressed for School Success* and why they think some schools have dress codes.

BUILD BACKGROUND Ask students if they have ever worn a uniform for school or for a club. Suggest to students that sometimes just wearing jeans and a t-shirt or dressing up for a party can also be considered a uniform if everyone dresses in the same way. Ask students why they think it might be important or beneficial to wear such uniforms.

ELL Invite English learners to discuss how students in their native countries dress for school. Suggest that English learners bring in a picture or drawing and discuss how their native dress is similar to and different from the way they dress now in the United States.

PREVIEW/ILLUSTRATIONS Suggest that students look through the photographs in the book. Discuss with students the different ways people are dressed in the photographs.

READ THE BOOK

SET PURPOSE Have students set a purpose for reading *Dressed for School Success*. Students' curiosity about dress codes, uniforms, and clothing in general should help guide this purpose.

STRATEGY SUPPORT: PREDICT/CONFIRM PREDICTIONS As students start to fill in their graphic organizers as they read, remind them that they can change their predictions based on new information they are reading.

COMPREHENSION QUESTIONS

PAGES 7–8 Compare and contrast the shoes worn by early Americans with those of young pioneers. *(Compare: Both wore shoes sometimes. Contrast: Early American students could wear their shoes on either feet; Pioneer children often went barefoot because they could not afford shoes.)*

PAGE 8 How did the culture of a farming community determine whether or not someone could go to school? *(If there was a harvest, farm children couldn't go to school until after they had helped with the farming.)*

PAGE 12 Why do you think schools made strict dress codes? *(Possible responses: It was easier for the schools, it was a sign of respect, it showed what school the student attended.)*

PAGES 12–15 What is the most important idea about dressing for school? *(Possible response: Different people dress differently depending on their school's rules and their culture.)*

PAGE 15 Based on what you know about your school, could you predict a new kind of uniform for the school? *(Responses will vary.)*

REVISIT THE BOOK

READER RESPONSE

1. Possible response: Dame school students wore dresses and petticoats or breeches with jackets. I wear jeans and t-shirts to school. Both kinds of clothes can be made from cotton. Shoes today have left and right shapes, not the same shape.

2. Possible response: I think they will wear clothes like we wear now, but they will be waterproof.

3. Uniform, chiton, shorts, breeches, doublet, petticoats, pants, knickers, jackets, neckties, socks, blouses, dresses, scarves

4. Answers will vary, but will focus on one particular generation of school clothes.

EXTEND UNDERSTANDING Direct students to read the captions on the photos and illustrations. Ask students what they understand about the photographs and illustrations without the captions. Then ask how the captions helped increase their understanding.

RESPONSE OPTIONS

WRITING Bring in examples of advertisements for clothing from newspapers or magazine ads. Discuss with students and then ask them to write an advertisement urging people to buy one of the articles of clothing on page 7 of *Dressed for School Success*.

SOCIAL STUDIES CONNECTION

Suggest that students research what Pilgrim students wore and then write and illustrate a report they can share with the class.

Skill Work

TEACH/REVIEW VOCABULARY

Review vocabulary words with students. Then give them the definitions and see if they can guess the vocabulary words. Have students use each vocabulary word in a sentence.

TARGET SKILL AND STRATEGY

COMPARE AND CONTRAST Remind students that a *comparison* shows how two or more things are alike and different; a *contrast* shows how two or more things are different. Suggest that students use a graphic organizer to help them compare and contrast the kinds of clothing they will be reading about in *Dressed for School Success*.

PREDICT/CONFIRM PREDICTIONS Remind students that *predicting* means to guess what will happen next based on what they have read already. Ask students to predict what they think dressing for school success is. Suggest that students write down their predictions in a graphic organizer and include details that support or change their prediction as they read *Dressed for School Success*. Remind students that making predictions can help them compare and contrast.

ADDITIONAL SKILL INSTRUCTION

MAIN IDEA Remind students that the main idea is the most important idea about the topic, and that this idea is sometimes stated in the reading selection and sometimes it isn't. Review a book students have recently read and ask them what the main idea of the book was. Then ask students to give you details that support their answer. Remind students that as they read *Dressed for School Success*, they should take down notes about what they think the book is about and what they think the most important idea of the book is. Suggest to students that they also write down any details that support their answers.

Name _____

Compare and Contrast

- A **comparison** shows how two or more things are alike and different.
- A **contrast** shows how two or more things are different.

Directions Using the Venn Diagram, compare and contrast girl's and boy's clothing.

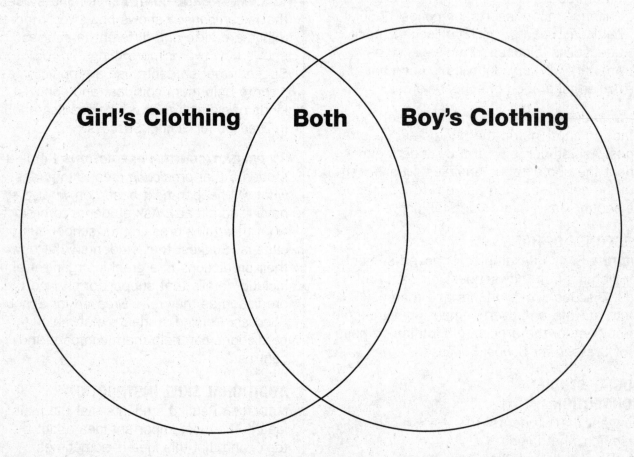

Girl's Clothing   Both   Boy's Clothing

A simile compares two or more things using the clue word *as* or *like,* and a metaphor does not. "She cries like a baby" is a simile because it uses the clue word *like.* "She is a baby" (if she is a big girl) is a metaphor.

Write two similes of your own. Then write two metaphors.

_____

_____

_____

_____

Name _____

Vocabulary

Directions Fill in the crossword puzzle using the clues and the words in the box.

Check the Words You Know

___cotton   ___festival   ___graceful   ___handkerchief
___pace   ___pale   ___rhythm   ___snug

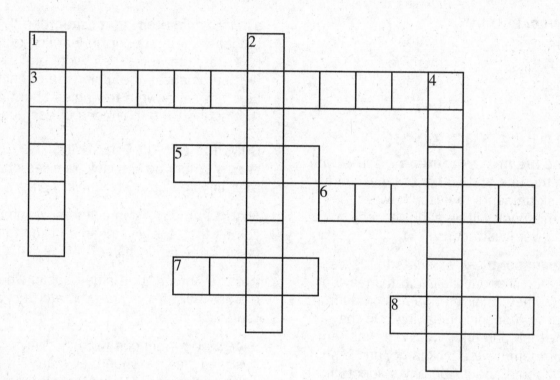

Across
3. soft square of cloth
5. a step
6. cloth made from white plant fibers
7. fitting closely
8. not bright

Down
1. a strong beat in music or poetry
2. beautiful in form or movement
4. an entertainment

What's in a Name?

SUMMARY This reader describes traditions for naming people in many different countries and cultures. Hispanic, Asian, Middle Eastern, African, Haida, and Maori traditions are compared and contrasted. The book also discusses changing names, nicknames, and exact meanings of names.

LESSON VOCABULARY

admire	custom
famous	mention
overnight	popular
public	twist

INTRODUCE THE BOOK

INTRODUCE THE TITLE AND AUTHOR Discuss with students the title and author of *What's in a Name?* Ask students to describe what they imagine this book will be about based on its title and cover illustrations.

BUILD BACKGROUND Ask students to discuss what they know about their own names. Do they know where their first name comes from? Does it have a specific meaning? Do they know why their parents gave them that name? Do any of them have a nickname, and if so, how did it come about? Do any students have middle names? more than one name? Do they like their names? If they could change their name, which name would they pick?

ELL Have students talk about their names. Do their names have specific meanings in their home languages? Do their home countries have any specific traditions for naming children? Do they use a different name in the United States from the name they received at birth?

PREVIEW/USE TEXT FEATURES Have students look at the headings and photographs and discuss how these text elements help organize the book. Ask students how previewing the headings can help them understand what the book is about.

READ THE BOOK

SET PURPOSE Have students set a purpose for reading *What's in a Name?* Students' interest and curiosity about names can guide this purpose. As students read, suggest they take notes about questions they have about the subject.

STRATEGY SUPPORT: TEXT STRUCTURE To give students more support in learning to recognize text structure, have them write one sentence that summarizes the main idea of each section, and jot down a few notes about details that support the main idea of each section.

COMPREHENSION QUESTIONS

PAGE 5 Whom do Hispanic families often name their children after? (*Catholic saints*)

PAGE 6 In many Asian cultures, which name comes first, the given name or the family name? (*the family name*)

PAGE 10 Among the Haida people, what does a crest indicate? (*where you are from and who your relatives are*)

PAGE 13 Do American women always take their husband's name when they marry? If not, what do they do? (*No, they sometimes keep their own name or combine their name with their husband's to create a new name.*)

PAGE 14 Why do you think Madonna changed her name from Madonna Louise Veronica Ciccone to just Madonna? (*Possible response: so people would remember it more easily*)

PAGE 15 What do you call a shortened version of a name? (*a nickname*)

REVIST THE BOOK

READER RESPONSE

1. "The entire name must be spoken." This is an opinion because some people may not mind if the meaning of their name is changed.

2. Similarities between both cultures: babies are named in a ceremony on the eighth day after birth. Differences: Jewish families often name their children after relatives. The Yoruba people use symbols in naming their babies.

3. Possible response: The success of the concert made the singer an overnight sensation.

4. Responses will vary.

EXTEND UNDERSTANDING Look through the book again, paying particular attention to the photographs. Discuss how the photos add to or take away from the meaning of the book. Look back at the picture on the front cover. Does that picture have new meaning once the book has been read?

RESPONSE OPTIONS

WRITING Have students write a paragraph about their own name. Do they think the name suits them? If not, what would they change it to if they could? If they were to change their name, what sort of a naming celebration would they like to have?

SOCIAL STUDIES CONNECTION

Have students look up *name* in an encyclopedia. Then invite them to find out as much as they can about the history of their names, using the Internet or library. Do any of the students have a last name that was a former profession, such as Miller or Smith? If so, have them research that profession. For more information, they can ask family members.

Skill Work

TEACH/REVIEW VOCABULARY

Review the vocabulary words. Then play *Vocabulary Master* with students. Give students three different definitions for each vocabulary word, including one that is silly. Have them guess the correct definition and then use the word in a sentence.

TARGET SKILL AND STRATEGY

FACT AND OPINION Remind students that a statement of *fact* is a statement that can be proven true or false; a statement of *opinion* is someone's viewpoint. Explain that facts can be proven true or false by checking in books; by observing, weighing, or measuring; or by consulting an expert. Give students several sentences, some of which are statements of fact and opinion, and have them label each accordingly. Then have students write their own statements of fact and opinion about any topic they choose.

TEXT STRUCTURE Remind students that authors use different *text structures* to help readers pay attention to certain details about the topic. Review the headings in the text. Help students recognize that the author wants us to compare and contrast these different traditions. Challenge them to think about how statements of fact and statements of opinion are organized in the book.

ADDITIONAL SKILL INSTRUCTION

COMPARE AND CONTRAST Remind students that when we *compare*, we look at how things are similar and different; when we *contrast*, we look at how things are different. As students read this book, have them notice similarities and differences in how different countries and cultures name children.

Fact and Opinion

When you read nonfiction, you will read some sentences that contain statements of **fact** and others that contain statements of **opinion**. Facts can be proved true or false. Opinions are statements of ideas and feelings. They cannot be proved.

Directions Read the following sentences. Write whether each one is a fact or an opinion and explain why.

1. The population of the United States is a blend of people from many countries.

_____

2. Spike is the best name for a dog.

_____

3. Chinese, Vietnamese, and Korean names begin with the family name, or surname.

_____

4. The more buttons there are on a button blanket, the more power a person has.

_____

5. Many American women take their husband's name when they marry.

_____

Directions Read the following paragraph. Then write three facts and two opinions on the lines below.

> Surnames and given names have exact meanings in different cultures. Margaret knew that her name means "pearl" in Greek. It's fun to learn about different cultures. Joseph's name comes from a Hebrew name meaning "he will add." Joseph thought his parents should have named him Zach.

6. _____

7. _____

8. _____

9. _____

10. _____

Vocabulary

Directions Fill in the blank with the word from the word box that matches the definition.

Check the Words You Know

___admire	___custom	___famous	___mention
___overnight	___popular	___public	___twist

_____ **1.** *v.* to tell or speak about something

_____ **2.** *n.* an unexpected variation

_____ **3.** *adj.* liked by most people

_____ **4.** *n.* old or usual way of doing things

_____ **5.** *adj.* of or for everyone; belonging to the people

_____ **6.** *adv.* during the night

_____ **7.** *adj.* very well known

_____ **8.** *v.* to look at with approval

Directions Write a short paragraph discussing names as described in *What's in a Name?* Use as many vocabulary words as possible.

_____

_____

_____

_____

_____

_____

Joanie's House Becomes a Home

SUMMARY Joanie is not happy when she learns that her family is moving from San Francisco to Boston. She doesn't want to leave her friends and all her things. When the movers arrive with all the belongings from their house in San Francisco, however, the new house in Boston starts to feel more like a home.

LESSON VOCABULARY

airport	curious
delicious	described
farewell	homesick
memories	raindrops

INTRODUCE THE BOOK

INTRODUCE THE TITLE AND AUTHOR Discuss with students the title and the author of *Joanie's House Becomes a Home*. Ask them what they think the book will be about based on the title and the cover illustration. Ask students to talk about what makes a place feel like home.

BUILD BACKGROUND Invite students to share whether they have ever moved with their families. Ask: Where did you move from? Where did you move to? How did you feel when you found out your family was moving? Did you want to leave? Did you miss your old friends? How long did it take before your new home felt like a home?

PREVIEW Have students preview the book by looking at the illustrations and the section titles. In particular, have them notice the map on page 7 and the floorplan diagrams on pages 12, 14–15, and 16–17. Ask students to think about how these text features give an idea of what the book will be about.

READ THE BOOK

SET PURPOSE Have students set a purpose for reading *Joanie's House Becomes a Home*. Students' interest in families that move and in making new friends should guide this purpose.

STRATEGY SUPPORT: MONITOR AND FIX UP Have students use a graphic organizer to track what happens in the story. They may wish to use a time line or a sequence-of-events graphic organizer. Have students note points at which they have questions about what happens and have them go back to the text to add to their understanding.

COMPREHENSION QUESTIONS

PAGE 6 How will the Chens get to Boston? How will their things get to Boston? *(take a plane; get driven in a truck by moving men)*

PAGE 8 How do the raindrops on the window of the plane make Joanie feel? *(sad)*

PAGE 11 What is the first thing Mrs. Chen does to make Joanie feel at home? *(gives her a plant)*

PAGE 12 What did Mrs. Chen use to describe the new house to Joanie? *(a floor plan)*

PAGE 18 What did Joanie's friends from San Francisco send her? *(a team picture with all their names signed)*

PAGE 19 What does Joanie's new friend, Kelly, like about Boston? *(the ice cream)*

REVISIT THE BOOK

READER RESPONSE

1. 1) They packed all their things into boxes. 2) Moving men loaded the boxes and furniture into a truck. 3) The Chens took a plane to Boston.

2. Possible response: She's unhappy about moving.

3. Possible response: indifferent, uninterested, unconcerned

4. Possible response: Mr. and Mrs. Chen's room, Joanie's room, Jimmy's room, living room, dining room

EXTEND UNDERSTANDING Have students comment on the illustrations in the selection. Invite them to explain how they show changes in Joanie's feelings. Invite them to explain the changes in the floor plan from page 12 to pages 14–15 to pages 16–17.

RESPONSE OPTIONS

WRITING Invite students to write a paragraph about what it would be like to move to a new place with their families, or write about a time they moved. Have them tell how they felt before they moved and include when they felt like the new place was home.

SOCIAL STUDIES CONNECTION

Students can learn more about how people feel when they move to a new home by going to the library or using the Internet. Have them look for stories about students who came to this country with their families as immigrants from other countries. Encourage them to think about how people gain things and lose things when they move to a new home.

Skill Work

TEACH/REVIEW VOCABULARY

Challenge students to write a short story that includes each of the vocabulary words. Have them read their stories to the class.

TARGET SKILL AND STRATEGY

SEQUENCE Remind students that *sequence* means "order." Explain that clue words such as *first, then,* and *finally* are often used to signal sequence. Invite them to look for these clue words as they read.

ELL Invite students to make a list of sequence clue words. Suggest they compare them with similar words in their home language. Have them use the words in English to retell the story. Encourage them to retell the events of the story in order.

MONITOR AND FIX UP Remind students that a good reader takes note when a text is making sense and when it has stopped making sense. A good reader also has strategies for restoring understanding. Challenge students to stop and ask themselves whether they understand the story every two pages. Have them keep track of what happens first, next, and last.

ADDITIONAL SKILL INSTRUCTION

DRAW CONCLUSIONS Remind students that a *conclusion* is a decision you reach that makes sense after you think about the details and the characters and what happens in a story. Ask them to consider whether the conclusions they draw make sense. If not, invite them to rethink their conclusions and draw new conclusions. Have them share their conclusions with the class and support them with details from the story.

Name _____

Sequence

- **Sequence** is the order of events in a story.
- Authors sometimes use clue words such as **first, next, then,** and **last** to tell the order of events.

Directions Read the following paragraph based on *Joanie's House Becomes a Home*. Then put the following events in the correct sequence. Write the letters on the lines below.

The Chens said farewell to their old house in San Francisco, California. First, the Chens packed all their things into boxes. Second, moving men loaded the boxes and the furniture into a truck. Next, the Chens went to the airport and flew to Boston. Then they arrived at their new house. Finally, the moving men arrived with all their things.

a. The moving men arrived with all their things.

b. The Chens went to the airport and flew to Boston.

c. The moving men loaded the boxes and furniture into the truck.

d. The Chens packed all their things into boxes.

e. The Chens arrived at their new house.

1. _____

2. _____

3. _____

4. _____

5. _____

Name _____

Vocabulary

Directions Draw a line from each word to its definition.

Check the Words You Know
___airport ___curious ___delicious ___described
___farewell ___homesick ___memories ___raindrops

1. airport   missing friends and family

2. curious   thoughts of things that happened in the past

3. delicious   told about, explained

4. described   place where airplanes take off and land

5. farewell   very tasty

6. homesick   drops of water falling from clouds

7. memories   eager to find out about something

8. raindrops   an expression of good wishes when saying good-by

Directions Write two sentences about a time when you had to say good-by to someone. Use at least two of the vocabulary words.

9. _____

10. _____

Kapuapua's Magic Shell

SUMMARY This story is about a kind old Hawaiian man named Kapuapua who loves to sail the ocean in his canoe. One day, he comes upon an island where he hopes to get water and food. The islanders will give him water, but no food, so he tricks them by making seashell soup. The islanders want some of it, but Kapuapua will share only if they contribute food to it. This turns into a big feast.

LESSON VOCABULARY

bakery	batch
boils	braided
dough	ingredients
knead	mixture

INTRODUCE THE BOOK

INTRODUCE THE TITLE AND AUTHOR Discuss with students the title and author of *Kapuapua's Magic Shell*. Ask students what they think the book will be about. Does the illustration on the cover give any clues?

BUILD BACKGROUND Ask students if any of them have been to Hawaii. If so, have them talk about what they saw and the food they ate. If students have collected shells at the beach, have them describe this experience to the class.

PREVIEW Encourage students to look at all of the illustrations in the book. Do the illustrations give them an idea of what the story will be about?

READ THE BOOK

SET PURPOSE Have students *set a purpose* for reading *Kapuapua's Magic Shell*. Remind students that setting a purpose helps guide their reading. They could think about how Kapuapua will get what he wants in the story.

STRATEGY SUPPORT: SUMMARIZE Help students understand that summarizing what they read helps them organize what happens in a story. For instance, suggest that students take a section of *Kapuapua's Magic Shell*, such as pages 8 to 11. Have them summarize what Kapuapua does to get food from the villagers. Then suggest that they summarize how this idea grows into a big celebration.

COMPREHENSION QUESTIONS

PAGE 5 Why were the islanders at first so upset that Kapuapua had landed on their island? *(They did not want to share their food.)*

PAGE 8 What happened that gave Kapuapua his idea? *(A coconut fell on his head.)*

PAGE 11 What did the villagers have to do in order to taste the magic soup? *(They had to add some food to the soup.)*

PAGE 13 What did Kapuapua teach the islanders to bake? *(sweet bread)*

PAGE 16 Besides the bread and the soup, what other things did they eat at their feast? *(roasted pig and fruit)*

PAGE 19 Kapuapua was treated like a thief at the beginning of the story. How was he treated by the end? *(like a king)*

REVISIT THE BOOK

READER RESPONSE

1. Possible response: They were not very friendly. They didn't want to share their food.
2. Possible responses: There are many ways to achieve your goal. Instead of getting angry, get creative.
3. Summaries will vary.
4. Possible response: Beginning: They didn't want to share their food. Middle: They helped Kapuapua make his soup. End: They treated Kapuapua like a king.

EXTEND UNDERSTANDING Have students think more about the lesson of this story. What is the lesson that the islanders learned? What is the lesson that the author wants us to take away from the story?

RESPONSE OPTIONS

WRITING Have students imagine they have landed their canoe on a deserted island. What would they do to find food and water? How would they make a shelter?

SOCIAL STUDIES CONNECTION

Have students research the islands of Hawaii. They should find out about its history, food, music, and dance. How did the original Hawaiians get there? What types of boats have Hawaiians used? Students can also look into the volcanic history of the islands.

Skill Work

TEACH/REVIEW VOCABULARY

Go over the meanings of the vocabulary words. Tell students to guess a mystery word based on three clues about the word. One set of students can make the clues, and another group can guess. Create clues for all other vocabulary words.

ELL Have students talk about a time they were invited to someone's home for dinner or a time when someone came to dinner at their home. Ask: What did you eat and who was at the table?

TARGET SKILL AND STRATEGY

DRAW CONCLUSIONS Remind students that *drawing conclusions* means making a decision after thinking about facts or details. Have students think about the following question as they read: Why does Kapuapua's trick work so well on the islanders? *(They are curious about the magic soup.)*

SUMMARIZE Remind students that *summarizing* is boiling down a story to its main points. To gain practice, have students summarize their favorite books or movies. Or they can take notes as they read this story and summarize it once they have finished reading the book. They should try to draw conclusions about the story's lesson.

ADDITIONAL SKILL INSTRUCTION

THEME Without using the word *theme*, remind students that many stories include one big idea, or lesson, about how people should act. Discuss the lessons in familiar stories such as *The Tortoise and the Hare (slow and steady wins the race)*. Ask students how that big idea provides a lesson about how people should behave.

Name _____

Draw Conclusions

- To draw a **conclusion** is to think about facts and details and decide something about them.

Directions Read the following passage from *Kapuapua's Magic Shell*. Then fill in the chart below. Write a fact about Kapuapua in the first box. Write a fact about the villagers in the second box. Write your conclusion in the last box.

Kapuapua continued with the story. He told the villagers, "As soon as the water boils, I will make a pot of magic soup." But, he told them, they could not have any of his soup. There was only enough for one person.

Soon the villagers asked if they could add some food of their own. Then there would be enough for them to taste. Kapuapua just smiled and kept on stirring.

Kapuapua picked up the seashell. He was the only one who knew it was just a regular shell that he found a long time ago. He dropped it into the water. A little splash jumped from the pot and landed on the back of his hand. Then he said, "Mmm, this soup is going to be great!"

Soon the villagers begged for a taste. Kapuapua told them they could have a taste if they added other ingredients to the pot. They asked what they could add to the mixture.

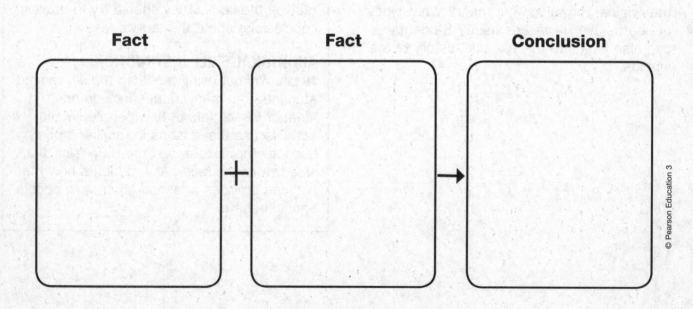

Fact   **Fact**   **Conclusion**

Vocabulary

Directions Complete each sentence with the word from the word box that fits best.

Check the Words You Know

___bakery	___batch	___boils	___braided
___dough	___ingredients	___knead	___mixture

1. Kapuapua made a _____ of magic soup.

2. The villagers added fish and vegetables to the _____ in the pot.

3. Kapuapua was pleased with all the _____ the villagers brought.

4. The villagers bought wonderful bread from their _____ .

5. The baker had to _____ the dough for a long time.

6. Kapuapua used to wear his long hair _____ .

7. When the water _____ , Kapuapua throws the shell into the soup.

8. The baker added raisins and nuts to the bread _____ .

Directions Write a paragraph about all the food at Kapuapua's feast, using as many vocabulary words as possible.

_____

_____

_____

_____

_____

_____

Bobby's New Apartment

SUMMARY This fictional reader tells the story of Bobby and his parents moving from a house in a small town to an apartment building in a big city. It shows how Bobby is scared at first, but then adjusts to his new life and home.

LESSON VOCABULARY

cardboard	feast
fierce	flights
pitcher	ruined
stoops	treasure

INTRODUCE THE BOOK

INTRODUCE THE TITLE AND AUTHOR Discuss with students the title and author of *Bobby's New Apartment*. Ask students to describe what they think the book will be about based on the title and the cover illustration. Ask students if they think Bobby's new apartment is in a big city or small town.

BUILD BACKGROUND Ask students if they have ever moved to a new place, and if so, how they felt about leaving their old home. Ask students to name some of the reasons that people move to new homes. Elicit some of the adjustments people have to make when they move to a new place.

ELL Ask students if their family has ever moved. If they answer yes, ask them to discuss the good and bad parts of their move. Ask all students to think about what they would pack for a move and what they would want to do before they left (example: say good-by to their friends).

PREVIEW Have students skim the reader, paying close attention to the illustrations. Ask students what they think the book is going to be about based on its illustrations.

READ THE BOOK

SET PURPOSE Encourage students to set a purpose for reading this book. After they preview the book and look at the illustrations, ask them to write down a few questions that they hope to answer by reading the book.

STRATEGY SUPPORT: PRIOR KNOWLEDGE Ask students to discuss what they know about the differences between living in a big city and living in a small town. Depending on the environment the students live in, ask the group if anyone has lived in the other kind of environment. If so, ask those students to explain what they had the hardest time adjusting to after they moved.

COMPREHENSION QUESTIONS

PAGE 4 What sentences on this page are clues to how Bobby is feeling? *(He looked a little fierce to Bobby. We don't even know anyone. Bobby missed his house and his friends already.)*

PAGE 4 Replace the word *fierce* on this page with another word with the same meaning. *(Possible responses: mean, scary, angry)*

PAGE 6 After the doorman, who are the next people Bobby meets in his new building? *(Hazel and Mrs. Low)*

PAGES 14–18 Name some of the reasons why Bobby decided he liked his new apartment. *(riding his bike in the basement; the playground on the roof; never feeling lonely)*

PAGE 17 What does Jose say that compares living in an apartment building to living in a small town? *(He says people in the building need to help each other.)*

REVISIT THE BOOK

READER RESPONSE

1. Possible response: to show that moving can be difficult; to show that apartment life can be interesting and fun
2. Possible response: House: only one family. Both: People help each other. Apartment: many families in one building
3. Possible responses: to mean "great," to describe a comic-book hero
4. Possible responses: He shows Bobby that people in the building are nice. He becomes Bobby's friend. He shows him around the building.

EXTEND UNDERSTANDING Invite students to look back over the book. Make sure they understand that it is realistic fiction, not a fantasy. Ask them how they know it is a fictional story instead of a nonfiction book. Have them name the main character and explain what makes him the main character.

RESPONSE OPTIONS

WRITING Ask students to imagine that their parents told them the family would be moving at the end of the school year. Have students write a paragraph discussing how they would feel. Ask whether they would be excited or sad—or both—and why.

SOCIAL STUDIES CONNECTION

Time For SOCIAL STUDIES

Ask students to use the Internet or library to find the population of their city or town. Based on this information, determine whether it is considered a big city, small town, or something in between. Depending on the size, ask students to name a comparable town or city located in your same state.

Skill Work

TEACH/REVIEW VOCABULARY

Write each of the vocabulary words on the chalkboard, and ask students to find them in the reader. To reinforce the contextual meaning of the vocabulary words, ask students how they can tell what each word means by the clues in the surrounding sentence(s).

TARGET SKILL AND STRATEGY

AUTHOR'S PURPOSE Remind students that the *author's purpose* is the reason why he or she wrote the story. An author's purpose can be to inform, entertain, persuade, or express a mood or feeling. After reading, invite students to discuss what they think the author's purpose was in *Bobby's New Apartment*.

PRIOR KNOWLEDGE Invite students to take notes while reading the book. Ask them to make a note whenever the book reminds them of their own lives. Explain that their own experience, as it relates to the story, is called *prior knowledge*. Suggest that they list the page number and then complete this sentence: "This part of the book reminds me of. . . ." or "This character reminds me of. . . ."

ADDITIONAL SKILL INSTRUCTION

REALISM AND FANTASY Remind students that a *realistic story* tells about something that could happen, and a *fantasy* is a story about something that could not happen. Ask students if they think *Bobby's New Apartment* is a realistic story or a fantasy. Then ask students to write two clues from the reader that support their answer. Examples: Bobby is a realistic boy, as described on page 3. The descriptions of the city and building are realistic.

Author's Purpose

- The **author's purpose** is the reason or reasons an author wrote a story.
- An author may have one or more reasons for writing. He or she may want to **inform**, **persuade**, **entertain**, or **express** a mood or feeling.

Directions Reread *Bobby's New Apartment* and then answer the following questions.

1. Why do you think the author wrote that "It looked like there were a hundred buttons" in the elevator?

   _____

   _____

2. What did the author write that made you laugh or entertained you?

   _____

   _____

3. Why do you think the author wrote about the basement?

   _____

   _____

4. Why do you think the author wrote that the first time Bobby rode the elevator it made his stomach feel funny?

   _____

   _____

5. Why do you think the author wrote *Bobby's New Apartment*?

   _____

   _____

Vocabulary

Directions Read each sentence. Fill in the blank with the word from the word box that fits best.

> ## Check the Words You Know
>
> ___cardboard   ___feast   ___fierce   ___flights
> ___pitcher   ___ruined   ___stoops   ___treasure

1. Instead of walking up twenty-one _____, Bobby took the elevator.

2. The pizza made a perfect _____ for their first night in the apartment.

3. When they came into the apartment, the floors were covered with _____.

4. Bobby thought the doorman had a _____ expression.

5. The painters had been careful that nothing was _____ by their work.

6. The boys found what looked like a key to a _____ while playing on the roof.

7. Bobby's mother brought a _____ of lemonade to drink with the pizza.

Directions Imagine you have been invited to play at the playground on Bobby's roof. Write a paragraph about it using as many vocabulary words as possible.

_____

_____

_____

_____

_____

Signs, Songs, and Symbols of America

SUMMARY This book gives students information about cultural icons of the United States, including Uncle Sam, the bald eagle, and the Stars and Stripes. Students will learn more about the creation, meaning, and importance of these symbols of freedom and how they are used in our society.

LESSON VOCABULARY

crown	liberty
models	symbol
tablet	torch
unforgettable	unveiled

INTRODUCE THE BOOK

INTRODUCE THE TITLE AND AUTHOR Discuss with students the title and the author of *Signs, Songs, and Symbols of America*. Ask students if they recognize any of the cover photographs, and if they know how each one relates to the title.

BUILD BACKGROUND Discuss with students what American signs, symbols, or songs they already know and why each one represents something about America. Ask students why they think a country needs symbols.

PREVIEW/USE TEXT FEATURES Suggest students look at the captions and the subheads in the book. Ask students how they think these elements help organize the book and help them understand the main idea of the book.

READ THE BOOK

SET PURPOSE Have students *set a purpose* for reading *Signs, Songs, and Symbols of America*. Students' curiosity about symbols should guide this purpose.

STRATEGY SUPPORT: TEXT STRUCTURE Have students do a text feature search. Hand out graphic organizers with the subheads: *title, heads, pictures, maps, photographs, bold print, captions, graphs*. Ask students to list the text features they find in the book. Then ask students to write how these external features fit into the internal structure of the book. When students are finished reading, suggest they use their graphic organizers to help them write summaries of the selection.

COMPREHENSION QUESTIONS

PAGE 4 What is the main idea of this page and what are two supporting details? *(The main idea is that America has many symbols. The supporting details are that the flag is one symbol and the bald eagle is another.)*

PAGE 11 Why would the cartoon encourage people to join the armed forces? *(Uncle Sam is pointing and looking directly into your eyes, making it seem as though he is asking you personally to join the armed forces.)*

PAGE 12 What details help you understand why the Statue of Liberty is such an important symbol? *(The statue is a symbol of the friendship between France and America. The crown represents the seven seas and continents of the world, the torch lights the way to America, and the tablet has the date of the Declaration of Independence.)*

PAGE 14 How does the heading give you an idea of what the topic will be about? *(The heading is about our nation's government buildings.)*

REVISIT THE BOOK

READER RESPONSE

1. Main Idea: Our country has many important songs written by people who were inspired by different moments in the country's history. Details: Francis Scott Key wrote the song that became our national anthem after witnessing a battle. George M. Cohan met a Civil War veteran who inspired him to write a song about the flag.
2. The headings tell the topic of each section.
3. unforgettable, unveiled, *un-* Answers will vary but can include *unlikely* or *unable.* Sentences will vary.
4. Answers will vary but should show some understanding of a battle scene and the inspiring effect of the flag waving.

EXTEND UNDERSTANDING Discuss organizational patterns with students, such as chronological or time order. Explain that signal words give students clues to these patterns. Suggest students brainstorm a list of words that indicate time *(when, then, after that time, first, next, finally)* and list the clue words they find in this book.

RESPONSE OPTIONS

WRITING Ask students to research the turkey and the bald eagle. Then have students imagine they are Benjamin Franklin and write an argument about why the turkey should be our national bird instead of the bald eagle. Suggest students work into their writings the facts they learned as they researched.

SOCIAL STUDIES CONNECTION

Divide students into groups and invite them to form their own country. Ask students to consider what kind of country they want to create and then have them draw a flag for that country, create a symbol, and write lyrics for a short national song. Share with the class.

Skill Work

TEACH/REVIEW VOCABULARY

Review with students the dictionary meaning of each vocabulary word. Then invite students to create clues for the words, following these models: Something that ___; this describes ___; and so on. Let students work in pairs to answer each others' clues.

ELL Suggest students make flashcards, writing a riddle for each vocabulary word on one side and the word on the other. Use the flashcards in class.

TARGET SKILL AND STRATEGY

MAIN IDEA Remind students that the *main idea* is the most important point about a topic. The main idea is sometimes not stated directly, but the details of a selection can give clues to the main idea. Have students read one section of the book and fill in a graphic organizer with the headings: *Topic, Main Idea, Supporting Details.*

TEXT STRUCTURE Remind students that *text structure* is a way to organize information. Recognizing internal structure can help students determine the main idea of a selection. Explain that the author structures this selection using description and definition. Have students jot down notes about descriptions and definitions as they read to help them recognize the text structure.

ADDITIONAL SKILL INSTRUCTION

FACT AND OPINION Remind students that a *statement of fact* is something that can be proven true and a *statement of opinion* is something someone thinks or believes. Point out that words such as *worst, too much,* and *beautiful* give clues that a sentence is a statement of opinion. Give students ten sentences, half of which are fact and half opinion. Invite students to identify which is which.

Main Idea

- The **main idea** is the author's most important point about a topic.
- Sometimes the main idea is not stated directly in a selection, but the details of a selection can give you clues.

Directions Read the following passages. Then write down the main idea and list two details from the passage that support your answer.

> Our flag has thirteen stripes to remind us of our first colonies. There is a star for each state. The colors all mean something. Red is for hardiness, white is for innocence, blue stands for justice. Betsy Ross sewed the first flag.

1. Main idea: _____

_____

2. Supporting detail: _____

_____

3. Supporting detail: _____

_____

> Francis Scott Key watched the British attack during the War of 1812. When he looked out after a terrible battle, he saw that our flag was still waving. This inspired him to write a poem about it, *The Star Spangled Banner*, which was set to music. This song later became our national anthem.

4. Main idea: _____

_____

5. Supporting detail: _____

_____

6. Supporting detail: _____

_____

Name _____

Vocabulary

Directions Use five of these vocabulary words to write a story about the signs and symbols of America. Then write definitions for the words you don't use in your story.

Check the Words You Know

___crown   ___liberty   ___models   ___symbol
___tablet   ___torch   ___unforgettable   ___unveiled

1. _____

_____

_____

_____

_____

_____

_____

2. _____

3. _____

4. _____

Caring for Your Pet Bird

SUMMARY This book tells how to care for a pet bird. Birds make wonderful pets, especially if they receive the right kind of care and feeding. This book describes what to do to make your bird happy and healthy.

LESSON VOCABULARY

bows	chilly
foolish	foreign
narrow	perches
recipe	

INTRODUCE THE BOOK

INTRODUCE THE TITLE AND AUTHOR Discuss with students the title and the author of *Caring for Your Pet Bird*. Ask students what they think the book will be about, based on the title and the pictures and captions in the book.

BUILD BACKGROUND Ask students if any of them have a pet bird. If so, ask them to tell the class what they have to do to care for their bird. Have them share their pets' names. Ask them if their pets are able to speak, and if so, what they can say.

PREVIEW/USE ILLUSTRATIONS Suggest students skim the text and look at the illustrations and captions. Ask the students what clues these elements give them as to what this book might be about.

ELL Ask students whether they have pet birds. If so, have them share the pets' names. Have them share with the class how to say *bird* in their native language.

READ THE BOOK

SET PURPOSE Have students set a purpose for reading *Caring for Your Pet Bird*. Students' interest and curiosity about pets can guide this purpose. As students read, suggest they take notes that might provide answers to any questions they might have about the subject.

STRATEGY SUPPORT: GRAPHIC ORGANIZERS Suggest that the students decide how they'd like to make a chart of the birds in this book. Guide them in setting up a column for each bird's name and a column for each description.

COMPREHENSION QUESTIONS

PAGE 5 Which birds can be taught how to talk? *(birds of the parrot family—parrots, parakeets, lovebirds, cockatiels, macaws, and conures)*

PAGE 11 Why does a bird need to have grit in its diet? *(Birds do not have teeth.)*

PAGE 12 What could happen if a bird is kept in a draft? *(It could get chilly.)*

PAGE 19 If a bird is not acting normally, what should the owner do? *(Call the veterinarian.)*

REVIST THE BOOK

READER RESPONSE

1. It can get lonely or anxious.

2. Things to Do Before You Bring Your Bird Home: get a cage, make sure the cage has several perches, get toys, get things for the bird to chew on

Things to Do After You Bring Your Bird Home: change water every day, change newspaper every day, give bird a bowl of water to bathe in, give bird grit, give bird a mineral block, keep bird warm and quiet, give bird 10–12 hours of darkness per day

3. chilly, warm; sentences will vary.

4. zebra finch; responses will vary.

EXTEND UNDERSTANDING Have the students look through the book again and look at all the photographs. Ask the students which bird was their favorite and why. Encourage them to find out more about that bird on the Internet or in the library.

RESPONSE OPTIONS

WRITING Have students imagine that they are going to the pet store to pick out a pet bird. Say: Write about how you decided on a particular bird and what you will name it. Describe your bird in detail.

SOCIAL STUDIES CONNECTION

Have students pick out one of the birds mentioned in the article and research it on the Internet or in the library. What country is the bird native to? What is its native habitat? Have each student report back to the classroom.

Skill Work

TEACH/REVIEW VOCABULARY

Ask students why they think the word *foreign* may be used in a book on birds. Ask them to look at the other vocabulary words and predict their use in a book about keeping birds as pets.

TARGET SKILL AND STRATEGY

CAUSE AND EFFECT Remind students that an *effect* is what happened and a *cause* is why it happened. Have students read pages 12 and 13. What could cause a bird to get chilly? *(cold drafts near the cage)* What could happen to a bird that is left in the sun? *(could become overheated)*

GRAPHIC ORGANIZERS A *graphic organizer* is a visual way to organize information. Have students make two columns on a sheet of paper. Have them label the right-hand column *Likes* and the left-hand column *Does not like*. Then, as they read the text, have them fill in things pet birds like and dislike.

ADDITIONAL SKILL INSTRUCTION

MAIN IDEA Remind students that to summarize means to boil down a story to its *main ideas*. Ask students to take notes as they read, listing the main points and supporting ideas for those main points.

Cause and Effect

- A **cause** is why something happened.
- An **effect** is what happened.

Directions Use *Caring for Your Pet Bird* to fill in each missing cause or effect.

Causes   **Effects**

1. Removing birds from their habitat can make them become extinct.

Why did it happen? → **What happened?**

2.

Why did it happen? → Zebra finches are kept in pairs.

What happened?

3. Most pet birds like the challenge of finding food.

Why did it happen? → **What happened?**

4.

Why did it happen? → Buy bird toys that are nontoxic.

What happened?

5. Most birds don't like the cold.

Why did it happen? → **What happened?**

Name _____

Vocabulary

Directions Fill in the blank with the word from the box that matches the definition.

Check the Words You Know

___ bows   ___ chilly
___ foolish   ___ foreign
___ narrow   ___ perches
___ recipe

1. _____ *adj.* from a country other than your own

2. _____ *n.* places to view things from high above

3. _____ *v.* leans forward to show respect

4. _____ *adj.* silly; not wise

5. _____ *n.* instructions for cooking

6. _____ *adj.* having a small width; not very wide

7. _____ *adj.* slightly cold

Directions Write a brief paragraph discussing how to care for a pet bird. Use at least three vocabulary words.

_____

_____

_____

_____

_____

_____

_____

A Whole World in One City

SUMMARY In this story, a young girl learns about the diversity of expression in Chicago's ethnic neighborhoods. The story supports the lesson concept of freedom of expression in a free society.

LESSON VOCABULARY

encourages	expression
local	native
settled	social
support	

INTRODUCE THE BOOK

INTRODUCE THE TITLE AND AUTHOR Discuss with students the title and the author of *A Whole World in One City*. Also have students look at the picture on the cover. Tell students that social studies is the study of how people live as a group. Ask: How might this story have something to do with social studies?

BUILD BACKGROUND Lead a discussion about how many Americans follow customs that come from other countries. Ask: Do you think that groups should enjoy their differences, or should Americans try to do everything the same way? Why?

PREVIEW/USE ILLUSTRATIONS Ask students to look at the pictures. Ask: What is the most important character doing? Have students read the heading on page 20. Explain that *ethnic* means having to do with large groups of people who are identified by their common culture. Ask: What is the purpose of this part of the book?

READ THE BOOK

SET PURPOSE Have students set a purpose for reading *A Whole World in One City*. Remind students of what they discussed in their preview. Help students by asking them to complete one of these sentences: I wonder _____. I really want to know about _____.

STRATEGY SUPPORT: MONITOR AND FIX UP Remind students that as they read a story, they should monitor, or check, their understanding of what they are reading. Tell students that one way to check is to ask questions. Model important questions that students should ask themselves as they read fiction: "Who is the story about? Where does the story happen? When does it happen? What happens in the beginning of the story? in the middle? at the end?" Remind students that if they can't answer the questions, they should use a fix-up strategy like rereading, seeking help from other people, or seeking help from reference sources. To help students use the strategy while they read *A Whole World in One City*, suggest that each time students turn a page, they write a question about the story up to that point and try to answer it.

COMPREHENSION QUESTIONS

PAGES 5–6 Why do you think Lily's dad wanted to show her Chicago? (*Possible response: He wanted her to feel good about staying there.*)

PAGES 10–11 Why do you think so many Polish immigrants settled in the same area? (*Possible response: They felt comfortable with people who shared the same customs.*)

PAGE 15 Read this statement: *Bobak's had one hundred different kinds of sausage.* Is this a statement of fact or a statement of opinion? Why? (*It is a statement of fact because it can be proved true or false.*)

PAGES 18–19 How is Lily at the beginning of the story different from how she is at the end? (*Possible response: At the beginning she did not like Chicago, but at the end she was happy.*)

REVISIT THE BOOK
READER RESPONSE

1. Possible responses: Fact: *Polish immigrants have been coming to Chicago for many years. Many people here speak only Polish.* Opinion: *It felt like we were in a city different from Chicago. Well then, you will love our next visit.*

2. Possible responses: Clarify facts and opinions, reread and review, or read on.

3. *il gi:* diary, Korean; *enchilada:* a rolled and filled tortilla, Spanish; *gracias:* thank you, Spanish; *chayote:* squash, Spanish; *mowimy po polsku:* we speak Polish, Polish; *kielbasa, kiszka, bolszewik:* sausages, Polish; *pagodas:* towers with curving roofs, Chinese; *karate, tai chi:* forms of martial arts and exercises, Chinese

4. Possible responses: No, Lily's family is not unique. Many people are interested in the cultures to be found in the United States.

EXTEND UNDERSTANDING Ask students to think about the neighborhoods in this story. Have them make a Venn diagram to compare and contrast all three.

RESPONSE OPTIONS

WRITING Have students write a letter to a pen pal from one of the neighborhoods in the story. They should explain how they express themselves through their family and community traditions.

SOCIAL STUDIES CONNECTION

Have students use an atlas, encyclopedia, or gazetteer to look up facts about one of the countries of origin in the story. Have them summarize and share these facts in small groups.

Skill Work

TEACH/REVIEW VOCABULARY

Distribute cards for each of the vocabulary words. Make additional word cards for *human*, *help*, *born here*, *peopled*, *face*, *cheers*, *nearby*. Reinforce word meaning by asking students to show the vocabulary word that best matches each word card.

ELL Give students vocabulary word cards. Have them sort the cards by the number of syllables in each word.

TARGET SKILL AND STRATEGY

FACT AND OPINION Remind students that a *statement of fact* tells something that can be proved true or false. A *statement of opinion* tells your ideas or feelings. It cannot be proved true or false. Turn to page 4 and find the sentence: *Chicago has many different neighborhoods.* Ask: Can you prove this statement true or false? How? Point out this statement on page 5: *That's much more fun, isn't it?* Ask: Is this a statement of fact or a statement of opinion? Guide students to see that this statement of opinion cannot be proved true or false. It is a statement of how Lily's dad feels about public transportation.

MONITOR AND FIX UP Tell students to check their understanding as they read by asking questions, such as: *What happened at the beginning?* Remind students that if they answer questions as they read, they will be able to tell the difference between a statement of fact and a statement of opinion. For example, as they read they can ask, *Can this statement be proved true or false?*

ADDITIONAL SKILL INSTRUCTION

COMPARE AND CONTRAST Remind students that a *comparison* tells how two or more things are alike, and that a *contrast* shows how two or more things are different. Encourage them to ask questions such as, *How are Pilsen and Chinatown alike?* and *How is Lily's life different from mine?* as they read this story.

Fact and Opinion

- A statement of **fact** is a statement that can be proved true or false.
- A statement of **opinion** is a statement of someone's judgment, belief, or way of thinking about something. Although statements of opinion cannot be proved true or false, they can be supported or explained.

Directions Write *F* beside statements of fact and *O* beside statements of opinion.

1. _____ Chicago has many different neighborhoods.

2. _____ It's much more fun to take the bus or the train.

3. _____ Mexican ice cream tastes better than regular ice cream.

4. _____ Pilsen is the largest Mexican neighborhood in any city in the country.

5. _____ The Polish neighborhood has better food than the Mexican neighborhood.

6. _____ It is better to feel like you're not stuck in just one place.

7. _____ The streets were filled with pagodas, fish markets, and restaurants.

8. _____ The Chicago Food Market has the best fish.

Directions Write your own opinion of what it would be like to live in a city with many different cultures.

_____

_____

_____

_____

Name _____

Vocabulary

Directions Fill in the blank with the word that best completes each sentence.

Check the Words You Know

___encourages	___expression	___local	___native
___settled	___social	___support	

1. She doesn't play much with other kids. She is not very _____.

2. Lily shopped at the _____ fish market in her neighborhood.

3. Lily's family moved to many places, then _____ in Chicago.

4. Lily's grandmother _____ her to keep a diary.

5. I was born in Chicago, so that makes me a _____ of Chicago.

6. At first, Lily did not _____ her family's move to Chicago.

7. When Lily saw the colorful neighborhood, she had an excited

_____ on her face.

Directions Use the words *encourages*, *social*, *local*, and *expression* in a short paragraph about your community.

_____

_____

_____

_____

_____

_____

_____

_____

Goldilocks and the Three Bears

SUMMARY This is a retelling of the traditional tale of *Goldilocks and the Three Bears.* While the Bear family is letting their oatmeal cool, Goldilocks enters their house. She tries their oatmeal, their chairs, and finally their beds, where she falls asleep. When the Bears return, they find her asleep in Billy Bear's bed. They wake her up, and she goes out to play with Billy Bear. In the end, the Bear family forgives her for disturbing their house.

LESSON VOCABULARY

crystal	disappeared
discovery	goal
journey	joyful
scoop	unaware

INTRODUCE THE BOOK

INTRODUCE THE TITLE AND AUTHOR Discuss with students the title and the author of *Goldilocks and the Three Bears.* What do the title and the cover art suggest the story will be about?

BUILD BACKGROUND Ask students if they know the story of *Goldilocks and the Three Bears.* Have them tell the story in their own words. What are the things that happen to Goldilocks in the story, and in what order do they happen?

PREVIEW/USE ILLUSTRATIONS Have the students look through the illustrations in the book. Do the illustrations seem to tell the story of Goldilocks in the same way that they remember the story?

ELL Have each student tell the story of Goldilocks, if they know it, or another fairy tale, perhaps one from their native country.

READ THE BOOK

SET PURPOSE Have students set a purpose for reading *Goldilocks and the Three Bears.* They could trace Goldilocks's actions or the sequence of events in the story.

STRATEGY SUPPORT: VISUALIZE Tell students that they should combine what they already know with details from the text to create pictures in their minds about what is happening in the story. Remind them to use all of their senses, not just sight, to help put themselves in the story, so that they can increase their enjoyment of what they read. Model: "On page 3, I read that the bears lived in a green and leafy forest. I know what a forest is like. I picture that the air smells sweet, and that there are lots of birds singing and animals running around. I think the bears must like living there." After page 8, ask: What kind of a girl is Goldilocks? What do others think of her? What details in the story help you picture in your mind how Goldilocks acts in school, at home, or with other children?

COMPREHENSION QUESTIONS

PAGE 4 Why was Billy Bear lonely? (*He lived in the forest far from his friends in town.*)

PAGE 5 What was special about Mom Bear's chair? (*It was covered in soft green velvet.*)

PAGE 9 What sort of crystal animal does Goldilocks break? (*a bunny*)

PAGE 17 What does Goldilocks do when the Bears find her in Billy's bed? (*She runs out of the house.*)

PAGE 17 Why does Mom Bear say that Goldilocks acts mean? (*She says she acts mean because she is lonely.*)

PAGE 18 Does Billy Bear stay angry at Goldilocks? (*No, he forgives her.*)

REVISIT THE BOOK

READER RESPONSE

1. Possible responses: Problem: Dad Bear is angry because of the damage done to the house. Beginning: The Bear Family goes out for a walk while their oatmeal cools. Middle: Goldilocks enters their house, eats their oatmeal, breaks a chair, and goes to sleep in Billy's bed. End: The Bears return home. Solution: They forgive Goldilocks.

2. Possible responses: hungry, excited, happy, smiling

3. Possible responses: Goldilocks discovers that she is in Billy Bear's house, that she's too heavy for Billy Bear's chair, and that Billy Bear's bed is just right for her. The Bears learn that someone has broken into their house, that a crystal animal and a chair have been broken, and that Goldilocks is sleeping in Billy Bear's bed.

4. Possible response: Goldilocks is selfish, while Billy Bear is forgiving. Answers will vary.

EXTEND UNDERSTANDING Have students think about what the big idea of the story is. What does the story tell us about respecting other people's homes and possessions? What details in the book support that idea?

RESPONSE OPTIONS

WRITING Have students write about a time when they were selfish and did something they regretted but were forgiven. Ask: How did it feel to be forgiven? Did you feel you learned something through that experience? What did you learn?

SCIENCE CONNECTION

Have students research as much as they can find out about bears. Assign each group of students a different type of bear, such as a brown bear, black bear, polar bear, or grizzly bear. Have each student draw a picture of the group's bear. Once groups have gathered all their information, have them share it with the class.

Skill Work

TEACH/REVIEW VOCABULARY

Encourage student pairs to find the vocabulary words in the text. Have them define the words and then work together to write a sentence for each word.

ELL Ask students to skim the story and write down any unfamiliar words. Suggest they look the words up in a dictionary and write the meaning in their notebooks.

TARGET SKILL AND STRATEGY

PLOT AND THEME Remind students that the *plot* is the sequence of events that take a story from the beginning to the middle to the end. Also, remind students that stories usually have one big idea or *theme*. Discuss with students what they think the theme is of familiar stories such as "The Tortoise and the Hare" (slow and steady wins the race). Have them tell the plot of the story by recalling the events in sequence.

VISUALIZE Remind students that when we *visualize,* we form pictures in our minds about what is happening in the story. Encourage students to try to visualize the scenes and characters in *Goldilocks and the Three Bears* as they read it. Have them try to activate all their senses: sight, smell, taste, touch, and hearing.

ADDITIONAL SKILL INSTRUCTION

CHARACTER Remind students that a *character* is a person or animal who takes part in the events of a story. As students read this story, have them try to decide what kind of character Goldilocks is. What is she like, and how do we find this out?

Name _____

Plot and Theme

- The **plot** is an organized pattern of events.
- The **theme** is the "big idea" of a story.

Directions Fill in the table below, which will guide you through a summary of the plot and end with your naming the theme of *Goldilocks and the Three Bears*.

Title _____

This story is about _____

_____
(name the characters)

This story takes place _____

_____
(where and when)

The action begins when _____

_____

Then, _____

_____

Next, _____

_____

After that, _____

_____

_____

The story ends when _____

_____

Theme: _____

Name _____

Vocabulary

Directions Fill in the blank with the word from the box that fits best.

Check the Words You Know

___crystal   ___disappeared   ___discovery   ___goal
___journey   ___joyful   ___scoop   ___unaware

1. Mom Bear made breakfast with one large _____ of oatmeal.

2. Goldilocks _____ from the Bears' house in a rush.

3. Goldilocks did not knock the _____ vase off the shelf.

4. The thought of oatmeal for breakfast made Papa Bear feel _____.

5. The Bears were _____ that Goldilocks was upstairs sleeping.

6. The _____ of the Bears' walk was to let the oatmeal cool.

7. The Bears made a big _____ when they returned home.

8. Goldilocks will be more careful on her next _____.

Directions Write a brief paragraph discussing Goldilocks's visit to the Bears' house, using as many vocabulary words as possible.

_____

_____

_____

_____

_____

_____

_____

Traditional Crafts of Mexico

GENERALIZE
PREDICT/CONFIRM PREDICTIONS

SUMMARY Readers learn about Mexican culture by exploring various traditional crafts. Readers can make generalizations about similarities among crafts and regions of Mexico. Topics are organized to support readers' predictions. Readers can compare their own prior knowledge of making crafts to the detailed descriptions of the text.

LESSON VOCABULARY

burros	burst	factory
glassblower	puff	reply
tune		

INTRODUCE THE BOOK

INTRODUCE THE TITLE AND AUTHOR Discuss with students the title and the author of *Traditional Crafts of Mexico.* Encourage students to comment on how the photo on the cover relates to the title. Ask students to predict what social studies topics may be discussed in this book.

BUILD BACKGROUND Discuss with students any recent crafts they have made at school. Or ask students if they have made any crafts outside of school. Have students describe what they made, what materials they used, and whether it was easy or difficult. Guide students to recognize that many crafts take practice to do well.

ELL Build background and develop vocabulary by encouraging students to discuss crafts of their native culture. Ask students to share native-language words related to crafts.

PREVIEW/USE TEXT FEATURES Direct students to look through the book and pay attention to the headings, map, illustrations, and photographs. Ask students to share with the class anything that is familiar to them. Encourage students to comment on what they already know about crafts or Mexico.

READ THE BOOK

SET PURPOSE This book touches on many different topics that students will be interested in. After previewing the book ask students to pick one topic that interests them the most, such as a particular craft, cultural group, or region of Mexico. Then have students write three interesting facts about their chosen topic as they read.

STRATEGY SUPPORT: PREDICT/CONFIRM PREDICTIONS Explain: Pausing while reading to predict what will happen next is a good way to check your comprehension. Practice this skill after students read page 7. Ask students to predict what the book will be about and write their predictions down. Students will benefit from hearing other students' predictions as well as other students' explanations of how they came to make their predictions. After students have read the book, discuss which predictions were correct or incorrect and why.

COMPREHENSION QUESTIONS

PAGE 5 What does the statement "The Maya civilization was at its peak" mean? (*The Maya were at the height of their glory.*)

PAGE 10 If a scientist found a blue pot and a green pot buried deep in the ground, which one would probably be older? Why? (*the blue pot, because the color green was introduced in the 1700s*)

PAGES 12–13 What are some differences and similarities between making a rug and making a basket? (*Both are woven. A rug can take 300 hours to make, while a medium-size basket can take less than an hour.*)

PAGE 17 Which craft is highly valued in Mexico? (*needlework*)

REVISIT THE BOOK

READER RESPONSE

1. Possible responses: colorful, handmade, traditional techniques

2. Possible response: The techniques might be lost forever.

3. Possible response: glass + blower = glassblower; responses will vary.

4. Responses will vary.

EXTEND UNDERSTANDING Pause when you arrive at the illustrated map on page 6. Guide students to recognize the many types of information shown on the map, including the location and names of states, cities, and bodies of water in Mexico, and the type of crafts made in the regions of Mexico. Ask: In what state is Mexico City located? What cities are on the Pacific coast? Where could you buy embroidered cloth? Where could you buy pottery?

RESPONSE OPTIONS

WRITING In order to teach a craft, you have to be able to explain how to do it. Have students write instructions or steps in a process on how to make something simple such as a mask, collage, poster, or hat. As a class, review time-order words for students to use in their writing.

ART CONNECTION

Have students make a mask to wear on their favorite holiday. Require that the mask's colors, decorations, and/or shape closely relate to the holiday. Give students time to share their masks with the class and discuss how they think it relates to their chosen holiday.

Skill Work

TEACH/REVIEW VOCABULARY

Play Memory with synonyms. Write each of these vocabulary words and their synonyms on separate index cards: *burro—donkey; puff—cloud, tune—agree, factory—plant; burst—blast; reply—answer.* Place the cards word-side down. Students then take turns turning over two cards at a time. Students earn points by turning over and recognizing words that have the same meaning.

TARGET SKILL AND STRATEGY

GENERALIZE Explain: When you read about several people, things, or ideas that are alike, you can make a *generalization* about them. As an example, read the first sentence on page 4; point out the clue word *many.* Group students in pairs. Assign each a different craft discussed in the text. Have pairs write a general statement about their topic. Next have pairs trade statements and evaluate them by looking at facts in the text.

PREDICT/CONFIRM PREDICTIONS Making generalizations and making predictions require students to look at details in the text. Stop and practice this skill after students have read page 7. Guide students to look for details that will help them predict what will happen next. Write students' predictions on the board. Then, as predictions are confirmed as correct or incorrect, pause and encourage class discussion.

ADDITIONAL SKILL INSTRUCTION

COMPARE AND CONTRAST Review with students the four main reasons an author may have for writing: to persuade, inform, entertain, and express. Emphasize that a writer can have more than one *purpose* for writing. After students have read page 3, pause and ask students to predict what they think the author's purpose(s) may be. Ask students if they think the book will be funny, serious, or sad. Record students' predictions to discuss during and after reading.

Name _____

Generalize

- To **generalize** is to make a broad statement or rule that applies to many examples.
- When you make a generalization, you look for similarities or differences among facts and examples in the text.

Directions Complete the graphic organizer below. Find facts and examples from the text that support the generalization.

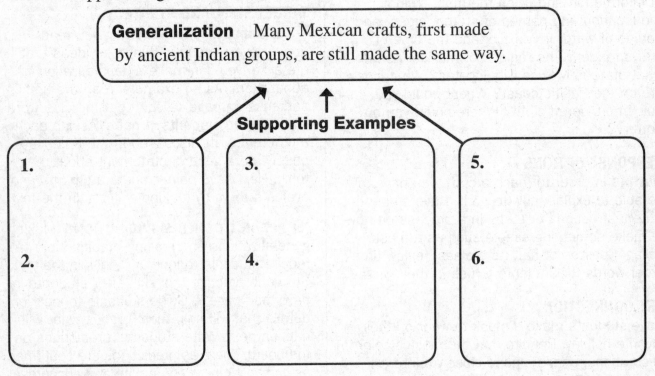

Generalization Many Mexican crafts, first made by ancient Indian groups, are still made the same way.

Supporting Examples

1.

2.

3.

4.

5.

6.

Directions Write a generalization about Mexican crafts. Then write three facts that support the generalization.

7. Generalization:

_____

Supporting examples:

8. _____

9. _____

10. _____

Name _____

Vocabulary

Directions Choose a word from the box that best completes each sentence.

Check the Words You Know

___ burros   ___ burst
___ factory   ___ glassblower
___ puff   ___ reply
___ tune

1. I can play a beautiful _____ on my flute.

2. *Arboles de la vida,* "trees of life," are known for their _____ of leaves and clay figures.

3. When decorating masks, people use a _____ of yarn to represent hair.

4. Many poor people moved closer to a _____ in hopes of getting a job.

5. Some Mexicans travel using _____ .

6. If you asked me if I would like to go to Mexico, I would _____ "Yes!"

7. The _____ sells his colorful vases at the market.

Directions Using as many vocabulary words as possible, write two generalizations about traditional Mexican crafts.

_____

_____

_____

_____

_____

_____

Story Prediction from Previewing

Title _____

Read the title and look at the pictures in the story.
What do you think a problem in the story might be?

I think a problem might be _____

_____

_____

After reading _____,
draw a picture of one of the problems in the story.

Story Prediction from Vocabulary

Title and Vocabulary Words

Read the title and the story words.
What do you think this story might be about?

I think this story might be about _____

_____

_____

After reading _____ ,
draw a picture that shows what the story is about.

KWL Chart

Topic _____

What We **K**now	What We **W**ant to Know	What We **L**earned

Vocabulary Frame

Word

Association or Symbol

Predicted definition: _____

_____

One good sentence:

_____

_____

_____

Verified definition: _____

_____

_____

Another good sentence:

_____

_____

_____

Story Predictions Chart

Title _____

What might happen?	What clues do I have?	What did happen?

Story Sequence A

Title _____

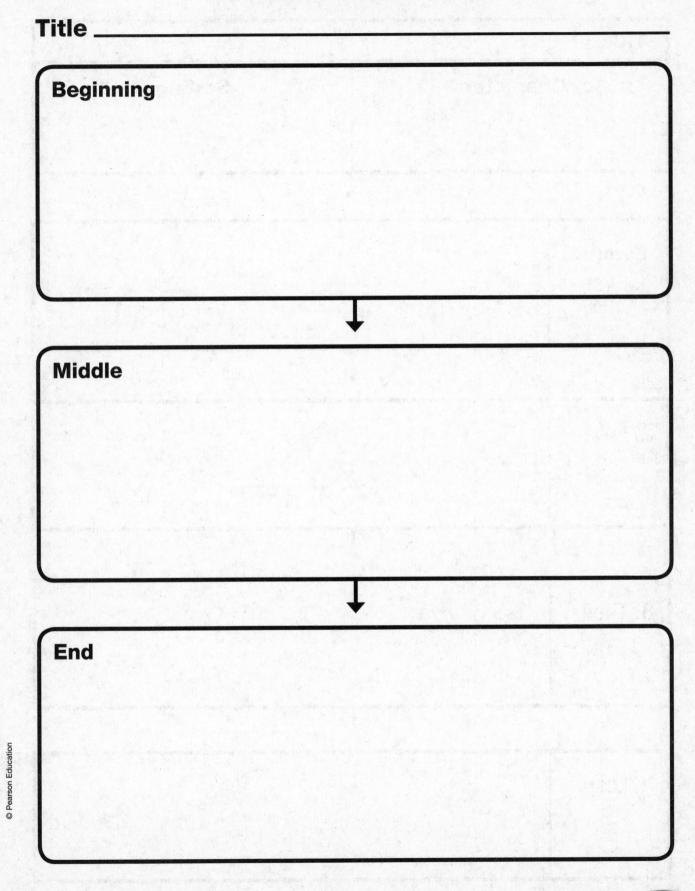

Beginning

Middle

End

Story Sequence B

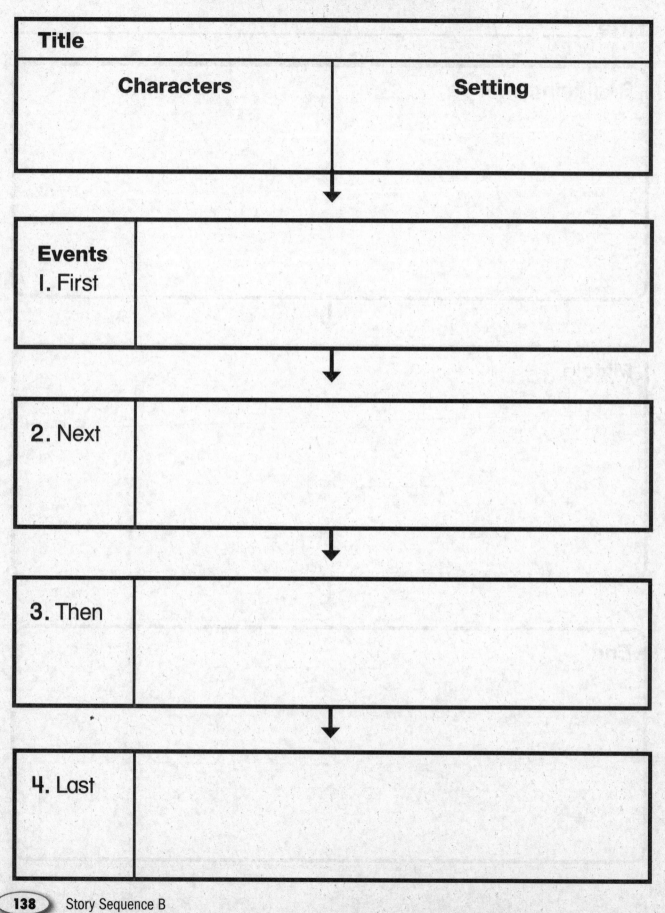

Title	
Characters	**Setting**

Events
I. First

2. Next

3. Then

4. Last

Story Sequence C

Title

Characters

Problem

Events

_____

_____

_____

_____

_____

_____

_____

Solution

Question the Author

Title _____

Author _____ **Page** _____

1. What does the author tell you?	
2. Why do you think the author tells you that?	
3. Does the author say it clearly?	
4. What would make it clearer?	
5. How would you say it instead?	

Story Comparison

Title A _____

_____

Characters

Setting

Events

Title B _____

_____

Characters

Setting

Events

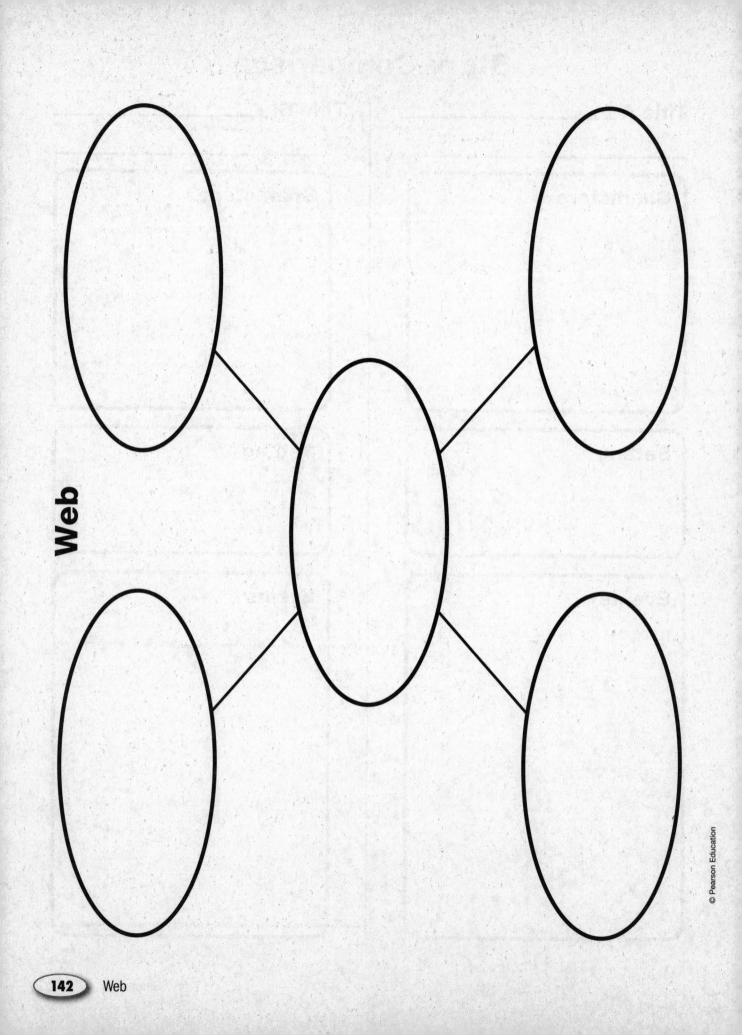

Web

Main Idea

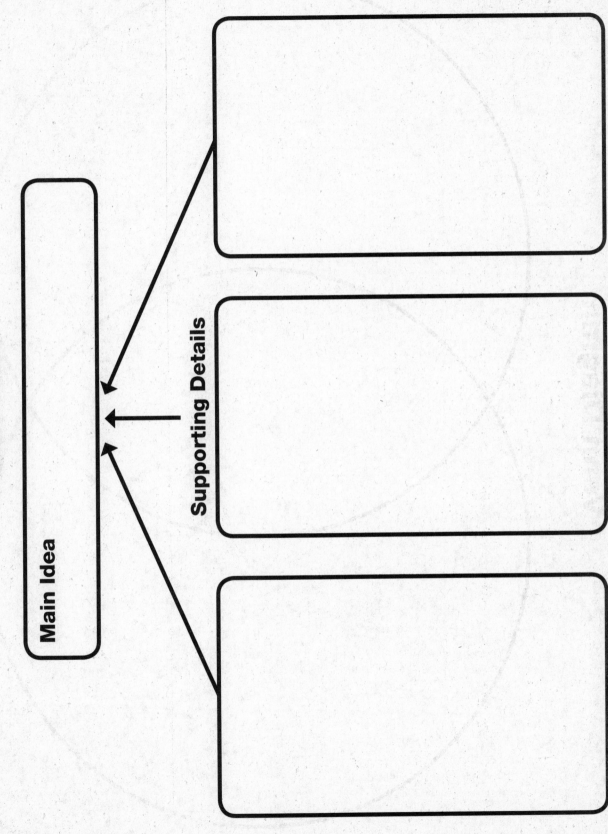

Main Idea

Supporting Details

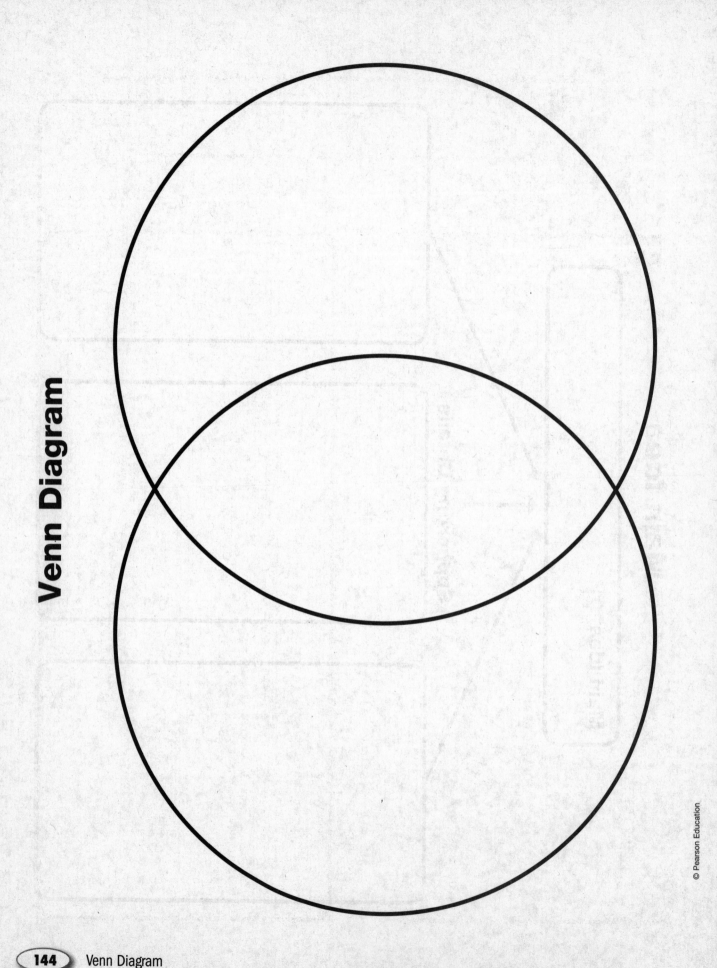

Venn Diagram

Compare and Contrast

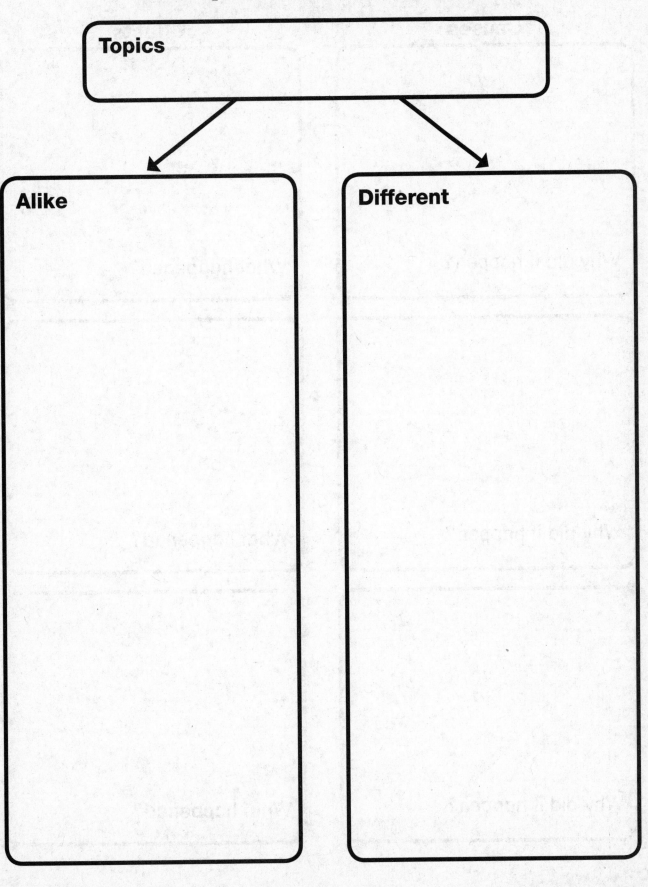

Topics

Alike

Different

Cause and Effect

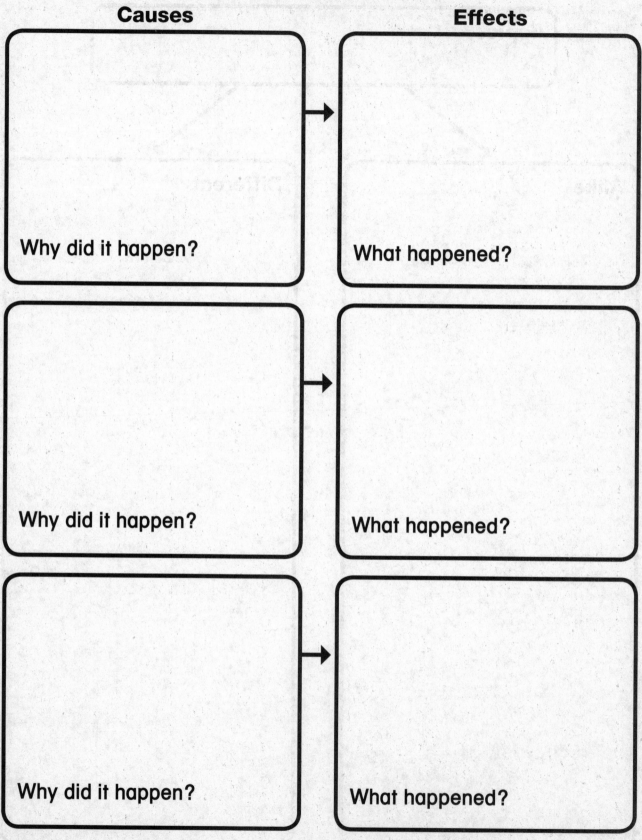

Causes

Effects

Why did it happen?

What happened?

Why did it happen?

What happened?

Why did it happen?

What happened?

Problem and Solution

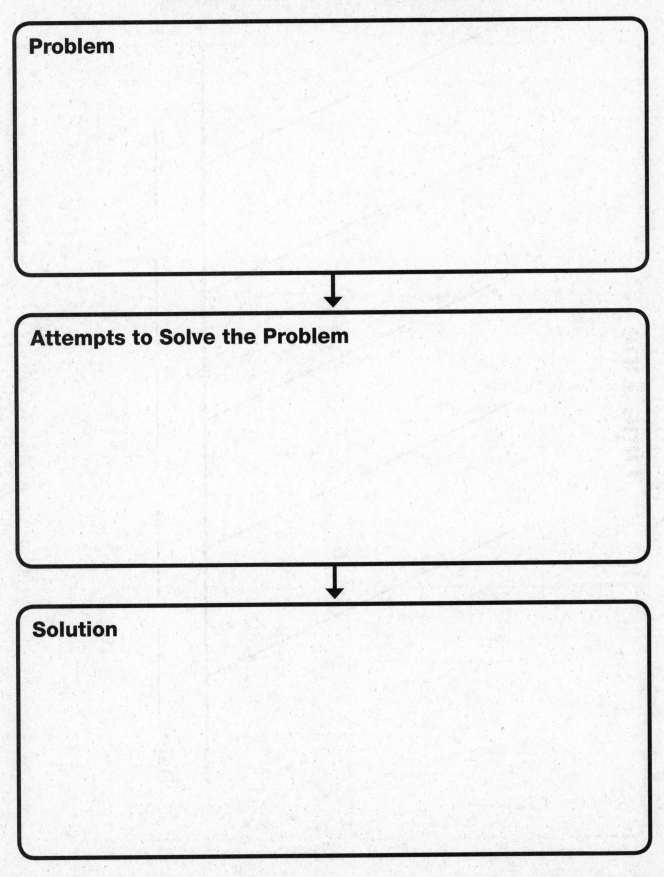

Problem

Attempts to Solve the Problem

Solution

Time Line

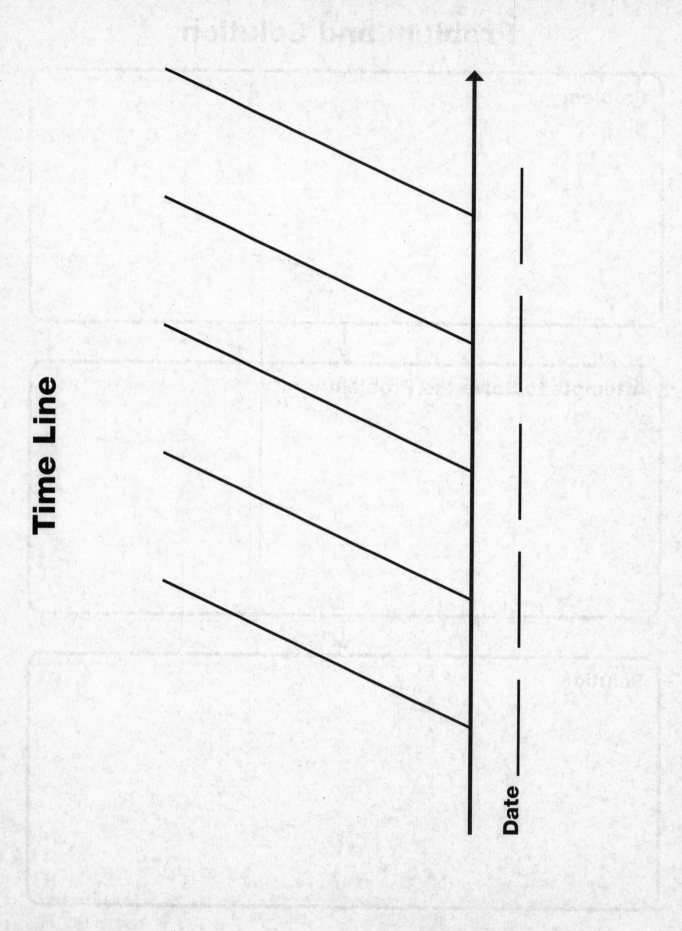

Date

Steps in a Process

Process _____

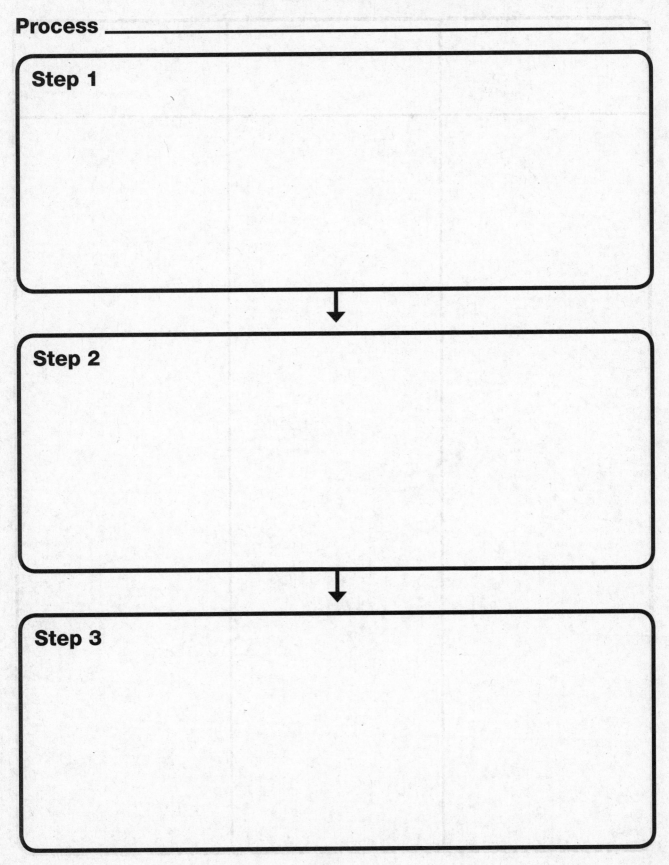

Step 1

Step 2

Step 3

Three-Column Chart

Four-Column Chart

Four-Column Graph

Title _____

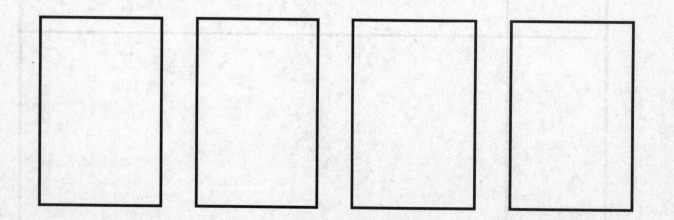

Answer Key

Leveled Reader Practice Pages

Salt Lick Boom Town p. 14

🌀 **REALISM AND FANTASY**

1. It's a fantasy.
2. animals bringing their newspapers to the salt lick
3. Animals are not able to knit and sew.
4. The raccoon builds a store.
5. in a boom town with people, not animals

Salt Lick Boom Town p. 15 Vocabulary

1. skillet
2. laundry
3. mending
4. pick
5. fetched
6. coins
7. spell
8. boom
9. spell
10. pick

11–13. Sentences will vary.

Let's Make a Trade! p. 18

🌀 **SEQUENCE**

1. People decide what skills or goods they have to offer in trade for skills and goods that they want. People meet and agree to trade, or bargain for a trade, or not have a trade at all.
2. Native Americans bartered animal furs for the cloth, thread, and tools the colonists had.
3. The students display their items to trade. They decide what they want to barter for. Students find items to trade or keep their own items.
4. The theater offered free office space to a local radio station that needed it in exchange for free advertising.
5. Mr. Smith could offer his business knowledge to help Mr. Jones in his carpentry business in exchange for Mr. Jones's building him a table. The Jones daughter could tutor the Smith daughters in math in exchange for a sports card.

Let's Make a Trade! p. 19 Vocabulary

1. carpenter
2. knowledge
3. marketplace
4. plenty
5. straying
6. thread
7. carpetmaker
8. merchant
9. marketplace
10. plenty
11. thread
12. merchant

13–16. Responses will vary.

Let's Save Money! p. 22

🌀 **SEQUENCE**

Possible responses given.

1–3. First, she set a goal. Next, she decided how much time she had to save money. Then, she decided how much to save each week.

4–6. First, Darla decided she wanted to save money to go on the school trip. Then, Darla made a savings plan. Finally, Darla opened a savings account.

Let's Save Money! p. 23 Vocabulary

1. downtown
2. quarters
3. college
4. fined
5. rich
6. dimes
7. downtown
8. dollar bills
9. rewarded
10. summer camp

Paragraphs will vary.

Earning Money My Own Way p. 26

🌀 **REALISM AND FANTASY**

1. F
2. R
3. F
4. R
5. F
6. realistic story

Possible responses given.

7. Andy wants to go to a concert.
8. Liz uses a computer.
9. Mr. Thornton is getting older and needs help.
10. Andy gets paid for doing a good job.

11–12. Responses will vary.

Earning Money My Own Way p. 27 Vocabulary

1. amount
2. interest
3. value
4. million
5. check
6. expensive
7. earn
8. thousand
9. worth
10. check

Sentences will vary.

One Chili Pepper p. 30

🌀 **CHARACTER AND SETTING**

Possible responses given.

1. she is adventurous; she's kind; she wants to help her family
2. curious about her new environment
3. excited to do what the people in her new setting do
4. Responses will vary.

One Chili Pepper p. 31 Vocabulary
Sentences will vary.
1. errands   3. bundles
   unwrapped   4. steady
2. excitedly   dangerously
Paragraphs will vary.

Birds That Can't Fly! p. 34

🎯 **MAIN IDEA**
Possible responses given.
1. flightless birds
2. Flightless birds differ from flying birds in many ways.
3. The bones of flightless birds are heavier than those of flying birds.
4. The feathers of flightless birds are different from those of flying birds.
5. A flightless bird's breastbone is different from that of a flying bird.

Birds That Can't Fly! p. 35 Vocabulary

1. hugs, snuggles   5. strikes, hits
2. paddles, fins   6. dress, groom
3. chilly, icy   7. nestles, holds
4. produce, cause   Responses will vary.

The Boy Who Cried Wolf p. 38

🎯 **CHARACTER**
1. Daniel
2. He is easily bored. He is mischievous.
3. He wants excitement. He wants more responsibility. He wants the villagers to notice him.
4–7. Daniel starts out feeling bored. He acts mischievous and cries "wolf" to get the villagers' attention. He gets scared when a real wolf shows up near his sheep. He promises never to lie again.

The Boy Who Cried Wolf p. 39 Vocabulary

1. unhappiness,   5. grower, farmer
   sorrow   6. pointed, signaled
2. smashed, smacked   7. surprised, jolted
3. trembled, shook   Responses will vary.
4. action, adventure

Katy's Last-Minute Book Report p. 42

🎯 **MAIN IDEA**
Possible responses given.
1. planning time well
2. It is important to plan your time well.
3. Homework, sports, and family activities take up a lot of time.
4. If you don't plan your time well, you might forget to do something important.
5. You need to plan enough time to do a good job.

Katy's Last-Minute Book Report p. 43 Vocabulary

1. group, set   4. separated,
2. huge, giant   sprinkled
3. recognize,   5. glossy, sparkly
   understand   6. try, strive
Paragraphs will vary but should use vocabulary words correctly.

Our Garden p. 46

🎯 **AUTHOR'S PURPOSE**
Possible responses given.
1. to show how much work is involved
2. to show that people working together can do great things
3. The author tells what they can accomplish by working together.
4. the heartwarming way the author shows how people improve their community
5. by trying to convince people that good things come from working together

Our Garden p. 47 Vocabulary

1. wealth   5. lazy
2. lazy   6. crops
3. bottom   7. clever
4. cheat   8. partners
Sentences will vary but should use vocabulary words correctly.

The Colonial Adventure p. 50

🎯 **DRAW CONCLUSIONS**
Possible responses given.
Fact: Colonists are drinking brown, muddy water that is not fresh.
What I Know: Drinking water that is not fresh can make you sick.
Conclusion: The brown, muddy water may be making the colonists sick.
Fact: Colonists try to make friends with native people, but they do not understand each other.
What I Know: Making friends with other people is hard when you do not understand them.
Conclusion: The colonists may find it hard to make friends with the native people.

The Colonial Adventure p. 51 Vocabulary

1. peg   4. barrels
2. steep   5. clearing
3. spoil   6. cellar
Paragraphs will vary but should include some correctly used vocabulary words.

Tulips for Annie's Mother p. 54

⊙ AUTHOR'S PURPOSE

1. CAUSE: Sue was moving
   EFFECT: made Annie feel sad
2. EFFECT: Everyone joked at dinner
   CAUSE: Annie's father now had a job
3. CAUSE: Annie's family had a farm
   EFFECT: they had food to eat
4. CAUSE: it took hours to get food at the store
   EFFECT: Annie's father was often late
5. CAUSE: Companies went out of business
   EFFECT: people lost their jobs
6. EFFECT: Annie's mother was sad
   CAUSE: she had no money to buy flowers
7. CAUSE: the stock market crashed
   EFFECT: stocks suddenly were worth nothing
8. EFFECT: Annie's family was happy
   CAUSE: Annie's father got a new job
9. Stock market crashed; banks and companies failed.
10. People lost their jobs; many people had to move.

Tulips for Annie's Mother p. 55 Vocabulary

1. g
2. h
3. f
4. a
5. b
6. e
7. d
8. c

Stories will vary.

Pictures in the Sky p. 58

⊙ AUTHOR'S PURPOSE

1. entertain
2. express a mood
3. inform
4. persuade

Responses will vary.

Pictures in the Sky p. 59 Vocabulary

1. narrator
2. antlers
3. language
4. imagined
5. poke
6. imagined
7. language
8. overhead
9. narrator
10. poke

Sentences will vary.

The First Year p. 62

⊙ DRAW CONCLUSIONS

1–2. He didn't pet the dog. He stayed by the door.
3–4. He said he would pet the dog later. He said he forgot something and had to go home.
5. Doug is afraid of dogs.

The First Year p. 63 Vocabulary

Definitions will vary but should reflect students' understanding of the word.

1. dew
2. fireflies
3. patch
4. budding
5. flutter
6. notepad
7. blade
8. hawkmoth

Sentences will vary.

A Day With the Dogs p. 66

⊙ GENERALIZE

Generalization: Most of the dogs are attached to Dana.
Possible responses given.
Detail #1: Many dogs race to greet Dana.
Detail #2: Shy Elvis sits on Dana's lap.
Detail #3: Dana spends time with each dog.

A Day With the Dogs p. 67 Vocabulary

1. melody
2. channel
3. surrounded
4. chip
5. blizzard
6. anxiously
7. symphony
8. supplies
9. bay
10. Sentences will vary.

Mount St. Helens p. 70

COMPARE AND CONTRAST

1. lots of trees, plants, and animals
2. no escaping steam, gas, or lava
3. fewer trees, plants, and animals
4. ash covers the city in thick cloud
5. Scientists monitor the volcano.

Mount St. Helens. p. 71 Vocabulary

1. buried
2. tremble
3. volcanoes
4. force
5. earthquakes

Possible responses given.

6. Areas far from a volcano can still become buried with ash if there are strong winds.
7. A volcanic eruption is nature's version of fireworks.
8. Before an eruption, smoke puffs out of the volcano like a chimney.
9. The surface of the lake was like a mirror.
10. Volcanic eruptions remind us of the heat and energy beneath Earth's crust.

Brave Settlers p. 74

⊙ CAUSE AND EFFECT

1. People today are more respectful of immigrants and the different traditions they bring.
2. They were different.
3. Her neighbors were from Russia, Germany, and Ireland and she didn't speak their languages.

4. Millions of residents were born in foreign countries and come from places like Latin America and Asia.
5. They were afraid they would not be allowed to enter the United States.

Brave Settlers p. 75 Vocabulary
1. struggled
2. complained
3. glaring
4. attention
5. looping
6. giggle
7. swooping
8. drifting
9. complained
10. attention

Lay of the Land p. 78
COMPARE AND CONTRAST
1. helps people find their way
2. uses satellite signals
3. used to find the exact location of something
4. measures earthquake waves
5. tells how far away an earthquake happened

Lay of the Land p. 79 Vocabulary
1. waterfalls
2. desert
3. peak
4. tides
5. outrun.
6. tides, waterfalls.
7. outrun
8. depth, tides, waterfalls
9. average, depth
10. tides, waterfalls

Fun with Science! p. 82
GENERALIZE
Possible responses given.
1. You can use binoculars to watch birds.
2. Watching birds is something zoologists do.
3. You can learn about the past by talking to neighbors.
4. Learning about the past is what archaeologists do.
5. You can use a telescope to look at the night sky.
6. Looking at the sky is what astronomers do.
7. Hobbies that kids can do relate to many different kinds of science. Science hobbies use many different kinds of tools

Fun with Science! p. 83 Vocabulary
Possible response given.
1. I like to work on my hobbies after I finish my chores.
2. Every butterfly has a label in my butterfly collection.
3. I keep my workbench for my hobby in the attic.
4. Collecting stamps is a really interesting hobby.
5. My hobby is darts, and I have my own dart board.

6. My hobby is to knit scarves and sell them to customers.
7. chores, customers, spare, stamps
8. attic, board, customers, label
9. chores, hobby, label, spare
10. attic, binoculars, spare, telescope

Women Who Made a Difference p. 86
FACT AND OPINION
Possible responses given.
1. In 1932, Babe went to the Olympic Games in Los Angeles.
2. online; in a biographical encyclopedia
3. Her memory and courage will live forever.
4. This is the author's belief, and it cannot be proved true or false.
5. She died at a young age of cancer, but her memory and courage will live forever. The first part is a statement of fact because it can be checked. The second part is the author's opinion about Babe's memory.

Women Who Made a Difference p. 87 Vocabulary
1. stirred
2. celebrate
3. medal
4. continued
5. strokes
6. drowned
7. current
Possible responses given.
8. I stirred the batter 100 times to make it smooth.
9. I love to celebrate Christmas by opening presents.

The Lost Dog p. 90
PLOT AND THEME
Possible responses given.
1. Sam's dog, Buddy, ran off to chase a rabbit and was missing.
2. Sam posted a missing sign. He threw out pieces of his clothes so Buddy would catch the scent.
3. Sam waited and was hopeful. The pieces of his clothing led Buddy back to him.
4. Do not give up hope
5. Sam did not give up hope, and Buddy came home.

The Lost Dog p. 91 Vocabulary
Clutched Echoed Gully Reeds Scrambled Valley
Possible responses given
1. I tripped and fell into the gully.
2. I scrambled to get to school on time.
3. When I had a nightmare, I clutched my stuffed rabbit.
4. The wagon rolled down the hill into the valley.

Dressed for School p. 94
COMPARE AND CONTRAST
GIRL'S CLOTHING: pocketbook, dress, blouse.
BOTH: jeans, sweatshirt, sneakers
BOY'S CLOTHING: suit, shirt, baseball cap
Answers will vary.

Dressed for School p. 95 Vocabulary
1. cotton
2. festival
3. graceful
4. handkerchief
5. rhythm
6. pale
7. snug

What's in a Name? p. 98
FACT AND OPINION
1. Opinion. A statement of belief, can't be proved
2. Fact. It can be proved.
3. Fact. It can be proved.
4. Opinion. A statement of belief, can't be proved
5. Fact. It can be proved.
Possible responses are given.
6. Fact. Surnames have exact meanings in many different cultures.
7. Fact: Margaret knew her name means "pearl" in Greek.
8. Opinion: It's fun to learn about different cultures.
9. Fact: Joseph's name is based on a name meaning "he will add."
10. Opinion: His parents should have named him Zach.

What's in a Name? p. 99 Vocabulary
1. mention
2. twist
3. popular
4. custom
5. public
6. overnight
7. famous
8. admire
Responses will vary.

Joanie's House Becomes a Home p. 102
SEQUENCE
1. d
2. c
3. b
4. e
5. a

Joanie's House Becomes a Home p. 103 Vocabulary
1. place where airplanes take off and land
2. eager to find out about something
3. very tasty
4. told about, explained
5. an expression of good wishes when saying good-by
6. missing friends and family
7. thoughts of things that happened in the past
8. drops of water falling from clouds
9–10. Responses will vary.

Kapuapua's Magic Shell p. 106
DRAW CONCLUSIONS
Possible answers are given.
FACT: Kapuapua has a plan.
FACT: The villagers don't like strangers.
CONCLUSION: Everyone can be fooled sometimes.

Kapuapua's Magic Shell p. 107 Vocabulary
1. batch
2. mixture
3. ingredients
4. bakery
5. knead
6. braided
7. boils
8. dough
Responses will vary.

Bobby's New Apartment p. 110
AUTHOR'S PURPOSE
Possible responses given.
1. to show that it was a big building
2. when Bobby wondered if people talk in elevators
3. to inform the reader how the garbage was taken care of
4. to show Bobby was scared
5. to inform the reader about apartment living

Bobby's New Apartment p. 111 Vocabulary
1. flights
2. feast
3. cardboard
4. fierce
5. ruined
6. treasure
7. pitcher
Responses will vary.

Signs, Songs, and Symbols of America p. 114
MAIN IDEA
Possible responses given.
1. Everything about our flag is symbolic.
2. Each of the colors stands for something.
3. The thirteen stripes remind us of our colonies.
4. Francis Scott Key wrote our national anthem.
5. He was inspired by watching a battle.
6. He wrote a poem that was set to music.

Signs, Songs, and Symbols of America
p. 115 Vocabulary
1–4. Responses will vary.

Caring for Your Pet Bird p. 118

⊙ CAUSE AND EFFECT

Possible responses given.

1. In the United States it is illegal to import birds from many countries.
2. Zebra finches don't like to be lonely.
3. Place interesting treats in different parts of your bird's cage.
4. Birds like to chew on their toys.
5. Make sure there are no cold drafts near the cage.

Caring for Your Pet Bird p. 119 Vocabulary

1. foreign
2. perches
3. bows
4. foolish
5. recipe
6. narrow
7. chilly

Responses will vary.

A Whole World in One City p. 122

⊙ FACT AND OPINION

1. F
2. O
3. O
4. F
5. O
6. O
7. F
8. O

Responses will vary.

A Whole World in One City p. 123 Vocabulary

1. social
2. local
3. settled
4. encourages
5. native
6. support
7. expression

Responses will vary.

Goldilocks and the Three Bears p. 126

⊙ PLOT AND THEME

Possible responses given.

Title: Goldilocks and the Three Bears

About: Goldilocks, Dad Bear, Mom Bear, and Billy Bear.

Takes place: in the house of the Bear family.

Begins: Mom Bear makes oatmeal that is too hot to eat. The family goes for a walk while it cools.

Then: Goldilocks wanders by their house. She goes inside to taste the oatmeal.

Next: She tastes the oatmeal, breaks their chairs and a crystal animal, and falls asleep in Billy Bear's bed.

After that: the Bears return and find the things she's broken. They also find her asleep in Billy Bear's bed. She wakes up, says she's sorry, and runs off.

Ends: Billy Bear stops her and says he forgives her.

Theme: It is best to respect the property of others.

Goldilocks and the Three Bears p. 127 Vocabulary

1. scoop
2. disappeared
3. crystal
4. joyful
5. unaware
6. goal
7. discovery
8. journey

Responses will vary.

Traditional Crafts of Mexico p. 130

⊙ GENERALIZE

1. The Maya made pottery.
2. The Aztecs made pottery, cloth, baskets, and metal work.
3. Today, there are Mexican folk artists.
4. Today, pottery is made without a wheel.
5. Today, people carve wood by hand.
6. People still embroider.
   Possible responses given.
7. Most modern Mexican crafts are colorful.
8. Some pottery is green, blue, yellow, and mauve.
9. Weavers use natural dyes to make colorful baskets.
10. Some masks are decorated with colorful feathers.

Traditional Crafts of Mexico p. 131 Vocabulary

1. tune
2. burst(s)
3. puff
4. factory
5. burro
6. reply
7. glassblower

Responses will vary.